THE PRICE OF MONOTHEISM

"mnemohistory" – how sources
have been read, as opposed to
what, in the light of modern
scholarship, they mean to say.
"Rather than asking how [X] actually
happened, it asks how and why it was
remembered." (p. 91)

THE PRICE OF MONOTHEISM

Jan Assmann

Translated by Robert Savage

STANFORD UNIVERSITY PRESS

STANFORD, CALIFORNIA

Stanford University Press
Stanford, California

The Price of Monotheism was originally published in German under the title *Die Mosaische Unterscheidung oder der Preis des Monotheismus* © 2003, Carl Hanser Verlag.

The translation of this work was made possible by the Goethe-Institut, which is funded by the German Ministry of Foreign Affairs, and by Geisteswissenschaften International—Translation Funding for the Humanities and Social Sciences, a joint initiative of the Fritz Thyssen Foundation, the German Federal Foreign Office, and the German Publishers and Booksellers Association.

Printed in the United States of America on acid-free, archival-quality paper

Library of Congress Cataloging-in-Publication Data

Assmann, Jan.
    [Mosaische Unterscheidung, oder, Der Preis des Monotheismus. English]
    The price of monotheism / Jan Assmann ; translated by Robert Savage.
        p.   cm.
"The Price of Monotheism was originally published in German in 2003 under the title Die mosaische Unterscheidung oder der Preis des Monotheismus 2003, Carl Hanser Verlag."
    Includes bibliographical references.
    ISBN 978-0-8047-6159-8 (cloth : alk. paper)
    ISBN 978-0-8047-6160-4 (pbk. : alk. paper)
    1. Monotheism—History.   2. Paganism—History.   3. Religion and culture—History.   I. Title.
BL221.A87513 2010
202'.11—dc22

                                                                2009014352

For Theo Sundermeier

Contents

Translator's Note

This book is a translation of *Die Mosaische Unterscheidung oder der Preis des Monotheismus*, first published by Hanser Verlag, Munich, in 2003. The German edition contained, as an appendix, reprints of five scholarly articles written in response to Professor Assmann's pathbreaking earlier book *Moses the Egyptian: The Memory of Egypt in Western Monotheism* (1997). The appendix has been omitted from this translation.

All notes and insertions in square brackets are my own. Quotations from the Bible are taken from the Authorized or King James Version.

THE PRICE OF MONOTHEISM

Introduction

At some stage in the course of ancient history—the dates proposed by the experts range from the late Bronze Age to late antiquity—a shift took place that has had a more profound impact on the world we live in today than any political upheaval. This was the shift from "polytheistic" to "monotheistic" religions, from cult religions to religions of the book, from culturally specific religions to world religions, in short, from "primary" to "secondary" religions, those religions that, at least in their own eyes, have not so much emerged from the primary religions in an evolutionary process as turned away from them in a revolutionary act.

The distinction between "primary" and "secondary" religions goes back to a suggestion made by the scholar of religion Theo Sundermeier.[1] Primary religions evolve historically over hundreds and thousands of years within a single culture, society, and generally also language, with all of which they are inextricably entwined. Religions of this kind include the cultic and divine worlds of Egyptian, Babylonian and Greco-Roman antiquity, among many others. Secondary religions, by contrast, are those that owe their existence to an act of revelation and foundation, build on primary religions, and typically differentiate themselves from the latter by denouncing them as paganism, idolatry and superstition. All secondary religions, which are at the same time book, world, and (with the possible exception of Buddhism) monotheistic religions, look down on the primary religions as pagan. Even though they may have assimilated many elements of primary religions in the course of a "syncretistic acculturation," they are still marked in their self-understanding by an "antagonistic acculturation," and they have strong ideas about what is incompatible with the truth (or orthodoxy) they proclaim. This shift does not just have theological repercussions, in the sense that it transforms the way people think about the divine; it also has a properly political dimension, in the sense that it transforms culturally specific religions into world religions. Religion changes from being a system that is ineradicably inscribed in the institutional, linguistic, and cultural conditions of a society—a system that is not just coextensive with culture but practically identical to it— to become an autonomous system that can emancipate itself from these conditions, transcend all political and ethnic borders, and transplant itself into other cultures. Not least, this shift has a media-technological aspect as well. As a shift from cult religion to book religion, it would have been impossible without the invention of writing and the consequent use of writing for the codification of revealed truths. All monotheistic religions, Buddhism included, are based on a canon of sacred texts. Then there is the further, psychohistorical aspect to which Sigmund Freud, in particular, has drawn our attention: the shift to monotheism, with its ethical postulates, its emphasis on the inner self, and its character as "patriarchal religion," brings with it a new mentality and a new spirituality, which have decisively shaped the Western image of man. Finally, this shift entails a change in worldview, in the way people make sense of their place in the world. The shift has been investigated most thoroughly in these terms, Karl Jaspers's concept of the "axial age" interpreting it as a breakthrough to transcendence,[2] Max Weber's concept of rationalization, as a process of disenchantment.[3]

I use the concept of the "Mosaic distinction" to designate the most important aspect of this shift. What seems crucial to me is not the distinction between the One God and many gods but the distinction between truth and falsehood in religion, between the true god and false gods, true doctrine and false doctrine, knowledge and ignorance, belief and unbelief. This distinction is struck and then erased, only to be reintroduced on later occasions in an exacerbated or attenuated form. Rather than speaking of a single "monotheistic shift," with an unambiguous "before" and "after," one could therefore refer with equal justice to "monotheistic moments" in which the Mosaic distinction is struck with all severity—the first and second commandments, the story of the Golden Calf, the forced termination of mixed marriages under Nehemiah, the destruction of pagan temples in Christian late antiquity—before being watered down or even almost forgotten in the unavoidable compromises that determine the everyday practice of religious life. This is discussed in greater detail in chapter 1. For now, I want to focus on the problem of temporality. The Mosaic distinction is not a historical event that revolutionized the world overnight, but a regulative idea that exerted its world-changing influence in fits and starts, so to speak, over a period of hundreds and thousands of years. Only in this sense can we speak of a "monotheistic shift." It does not coincide in any datable way with the Mosaic distinction, and certainly not with the biographical particulars of any historical "man Moses."

Before this shift there were only tribal and "polytheistic" cult and national religions, which had evolved over time; afterwards, new religions emerged to rival and increasingly supplant these historically evolved religions, several of which still survive in various cultures today. These new religions are all monotheisms, religions of the book (or revealed religions), and world religions, notwithstanding possible quibbles about whether Buddhism is really monotheistic, whether Judaism is really a world religion, and even whether Christianity is really monotheistic and a religion of the book. What all of these religions have in common is an emphatic concept of truth. They all rest on a distinction between true and false religion, proclaiming a truth that does not stand in a complementary relationship to other truths, but consigns all traditional or rival truths to the realm of falsehood. This exclusive truth is something genuinely new, and its novel, exclusive and exclusionary character is clearly reflected in the manner in which it is communicated and codified. It claims to have been revealed to humankind once and for all, since no path of merely human fashioning could have led from the experiences accumulated over countless generations to this goal; and it has been deposited in a canon of sacred texts, since no cult or rite would have been capable of preserving this revealed truth down the ages. From the world-disclosing force of this truth, the new or secondary religions draw the antagonistic energy that allows them to recognize and condemn falsehood, and to expound the truth in a normative edifice of guidelines, dogmas, behavioral precepts, and salvational doctrines. The truth derives its depth, its clear contours, and its capacity to orient and direct action from this antagonistic energy, and from the sure knowledge of what is incompatible with the truth. These new religions can therefore perhaps be characterized most adequately by the term "counterreligion." For these religions, and for these religions alone, the truth to be proclaimed comes with an enemy to be fought. Only they know of heretics and pagans, false doctrine, sects, superstition, idolatry, magic, ignorance, unbelief, heresy, and whatever other terms have been coined to designate what they denounce, persecute and proscribe as manifestations of untruth.

This book does not aim to provide an exhaustive account of the shift from polytheism to monotheism, from primary to secondary religions, that I have just described, but rather to clarify and further develop the position I advanced in my book *Moses the Egyptian* by confronting it with a number of critical responses and objections.[4] It is not my intention, however, to augment or defend that book, let alone to write a sequel. I want instead to deal in a more concentrated and comprehensive fashion with questions that concerned me only at the margins of the book or at the margins of my mind whilst writing it, but which the critical reception of that book first showed me to have been its central theses and themes. Literary theory has taught us to distinguish between the "authorial intention" of a text and its "meaning." As the author of *Moses the Egyptian*, I have been able to experience the legitimacy of that distinction firsthand. Only in the critical reception accorded the book did the thesis of the Mosaic distinction emerge, to my own surprise, as its semantic core, its chief concern. The book was almost universally understood as a contribution to the critique of religion, if not as a frontal attack on monotheism in general and/or Christianity in particular. Initially, I thought to defend myself against this reading by stating that such had never been my intention. I had set out instead to illuminate a previously obscure chapter in the history of the reception of Egypt in the West. The rage for all things Egyptian sparked in the Renaissance by the rediscovery of the *Corpus Hermeticum*, the hieroglyphic books of Horapollon, and the Roman obelisks, was widely known and comparatively well researched; likewise the eighteenth-century fascination with Egypt, with its sphinxes, obelisks, pyramids, and Masonic mysteries; and, above all, the "Egyptomania" that swept through Europe in the nineteenth century following the Napoleonic expedition to Egypt and the volumes of the *Description de l'Egypte* that resulted from it. All but unknown, however, was the episode in the seventeenth and eighteenth centuries that centered on the figure of Moses the Egyptian, culminating in the audacious idea that biblical monotheism has its roots in Egypt and represents a transcodification of the Egyptian mysteries. I wanted to retrace this newly discovered chapter in the history of the memory of Egypt in the West, from its ancient origins right down to its present-day consequences; and it may well be that, carried away by the exhilaration of discovery, I overstated my case. In essence, however, I wanted to attempt a historical or "mnemohistorical" reconstruction, not to embroil myself in theological controversy.

I have since come to realize that this argument is completely beside the point. What counts here is not the "subjectively intended meaning," whatever that may have been, but the potential meaning contained in a text, as it comes to be released through different readings and actualized in the interaction between text and reader—an insight, incidentally, that is entirely consistent with the methodological approach of a "mnemohistory" trialled in the book in question. For I, too, did not ask how biblical and other texts were subjectively intended, but rather what semantic potentials they were able to release in their readers. After five years or so of extremely lively debate surrounding *Moses the Egyptian*, I am thus grateful to take the opportunity to engage with the potential meanings that different readings have helped to crystallize. I would like, above all, to address the questions provoked by the concept of the Mosaic distinction.

My book has come under fire on two fronts. Some rebuke me for having introduced the Mosaic distinction, others for wanting to do away with it. In the first case, it is objected that I impute to the biblical religion (if I can summarize the ancient Israelite, Jewish, and Christian religions under that term) a distinction, and with it an exclusionary tendency, that is foreign to its nature; in the second case, it is objected, on the contrary, that I call into question a distinction that is constitutive for biblical religion, as well as for all the Western values that are based on it. Both objections, although diametrically opposed to each other, tar me with the brush of anti-Semitism: one sees an implicit intolerance in the concept of the Mosaic distinction; the other sees, in the demand that it be rescinded, a call for a return to Egypt, a plea for polytheism, cosmotheism, and a reenchantment

of the world. Rolf Rendtorff argues "that there is no Mosaic distinction
. . . in the Bible," hence that I have foisted on the Bible a construction
that is quite alien to it.[5] The Mosaic distinction is rather, as Klaus Koch
insists, "an antithesis borrowed from modern theories of religion. . . . [I]s
it at all suited to fundamental definitions of essence?" The transitions that
took place were actually fluid; polytheism and monotheism overlapped
in many areas, and their neat separation for analytic purposes flies in the
face of historical reality. The Mosaic distinction is a theoretical construct
without foundation in "real history, with its political, economic and social
factors."[6] Erich Zenger and Gerhard Kaiser go a step further when they
see this construct designating a kind of fall from grace. "According to
Assmann," writes Zenger, "the Mosaic distinction is nothing less than the
original sin of religious and cultural history. From an Egyptian perspective, it looks as if sin first came into the world with the Mosaic distinction."[7] If it is thus historically untenable to impute the Mosaic distinction
(between true and false religion) to monotheistic religion, then it is also
theologically dubious to call this distinction into question and to urge that
it be revoked. "Jan Assmann," writes Karl-Josef Kuchel, "wants to replace
biblical monotheism with cosmotheism. He thereby places himself in a
tradition that he himself has described with the keywords 'alchemy, cab-
bala, hermeticism, neo-Platonism, Spinozism, deism and pantheism.'"[8]
Erich Zenger ascribes to me the "fundamental claim" that "[t]his [Mosaic]
distinction has brought so much suffering and violence into the world that
it ought finally to be done away with. The price that human history has
had to pay for it to date is simply too high."[9]

These are weighty objections. They are not without justification,
as I am forced to admit with regard to several passages of my text, and
they warrant scrupulous examination. Moreover, they bear on problems
that were not entirely clear to me at the time I wrote *Moses the Egyptian*.
Indeed, I must confess that some points are still unclear to me today, albeit
not *in puncto* "anti-Semitism." It is all the more important to me, then,
that I add my own voice to the debate. Nothing could lie further from my
intention than to want to replace biblical monotheism, my intellectual and
spiritual patrimony, with a cosmotheism that I have now spent decades of
research exploring, although I am also aware that scholarly research of this

nature cannot be carried out without a modicum of empathy and simple respect.

This book sets out, not only to respond to objections raised by my critics in discussions, reviews, and letters, but also to engage with objections that have crossed my own mind over the years. In addition, they outline points where I believe myself to have advanced beyond the views I put forward four years ago. In what follows, I nonetheless seek to remain strictly within the thematic confines of my book on Moses. I have my critics to thank for whatever else I may have learned since it was published. I feel the critical reception afforded the book in so many diverse disciplines to be a great gift, one made all the more welcome to me by my own unfamiliarity with the terrain of most of the disciplines in whose preserves I have so impudently poached.

CHAPTER I

The Mosaic Distinction and the Problem of Intolerance

How Many Religions Stand Behind the Old Testament?

The shift from primary to secondary religion takes place in the Bible itself. Not one religion but two stand behind the books of the Old Testament. One scarcely differs from the primary religions that coexisted with it at the time in its adoration of a supreme god who dominates and far excels the other gods, without, however, excluding them in any way, a god who, as creator of the world and everything in it, cares for his creatures, increases the fertility of the flocks and fields, tames the elements, and directs the destiny of his people. The books and textual layers ascribed to the "priestly" traditional and redactional line are particularly shaped by this religion. The other religion, by contrast, sharply distinguishes itself from the religions of its environment by demanding that its One God be worshipped to the exclusion of all others, by banning the production of images, and by making divine favor depend less on sacrificial offerings and rites than on the righteous conduct of the individual and the observance of god-given, scripturally fixed laws. This religion is on display in the prophetic books, as well as in the texts and textual layers of the "Deuteronomic" line of tradition. As its name suggests, this "Deuteronomic" line has its center in Deuteronomy, the fifth book of Moses. This book breathes an unmistakably didactic and homiletic spirit that also animates other books and a specific redactional stratum. The texts ascribed to the priestly tradition lack a clear center, such as that represented by Deuteronomy, instead being dispersed throughout the first four books of Moses. Despite that, they have an all the more conspicuous center in the temple of Jerusalem. These texts belong to the cult of the temple and are addressed to a professional sacerdotal caste of readers, whereas the Deuteronomical tradition is pitched at a much wider audience. "The Deuteronomium," writes Gerhard von Rad, "has something about it that speaks directly to the heart; but it also satisfies the head through its continual willingness to explain itself. In short, it is perfectly adapted to its readers or listeners and their capacity for theological understanding. This vibrant will to interpretation is entirely missing from the writings of the priests. Their task was essentially limited to compiling, selecting and theologically classifying the relevant material."[1] Whereas the priestly writings constitute a manual that serves as a foundation for the temple cult, the Deuteronomium is a prescriptive textbook and guidebook that purports to lay the foundation for the practical and social life of the entire community. Over and above these stylistic and functional differences, however, the two lines of tradition appear to derive from two different types of religious experience. Whereas the religion associated with the priestly writings aims to make its people at home in the world, to integrate all things human into the divine order of nature, the religion that announces itself in the Deuteronomic tradition aims to transcend the world, to release its people from the constraints of this world by binding them to the otherworldly order of the law. One religion requires its people to turn towards the world in rituals of cult and sacrifice, giving their rapt assent to the divine order of creation; the other demands, above all, that they turn away from the world by assiduously studying the writings in which god's will and truth have been deposited.

These two religions are not just placed side by side in the Hebrew Bible. Rather, they stand opposed to each other in a relationship of tension, since one envisages precisely what the other negates. That this antagonism does not break out into open contradiction is due to the fact that neither religion unfolds in its full purity and rigor in the writings of the Old Testament. The archaic, polytheistic religion that seeks to make its votaries at home in the world is accessible to us only in fragments, having been painted over by the monotheistic redaction. It cannot be reconstructed in anything more than broad outline, with the help of numerous parallels drawn from neighboring religions. The post-archaic, monotheistic religion of world-redemption, for its part, is evident only as a general tendency in the books of the Old Testament, and does not come to full expression, in the severity with which it denounces other religions as idolatrous, until the writings of rabbinical Judaism and patristic Christianity that build upon those books. In the Hebrew Bible, both religions are able to coexist in this state of nonsimultaneous simultaneity, of a "no longer" and a "not yet." Indeed, this highly charged antagonism within the Bible undoubtedly represents one of the secrets of its worldwide success.

In its relation to two quite different forms of religion—one polytheistic, the other monotheistic; one turned towards the world, the other turned away from it; one a cult religion, the other a religion of the book— the Hebrew Bible resembles a picture puzzle: first one picture, then another moves into the foreground, depending on how we look at it. Neither of these two readings can claim exclusive validity. Those who read the Bible against the background of religious history and present it, on the basis of numerous parallels, as a Middle Eastern religion like any other, as does Bernhard Lang in his recent book *Jahwe der biblische Gott: Ein Porträt* (Yahweh the Biblical God: A Portrait),[2] prove no less guilty of one-sidedness than those who read it in the light of its reception history, as I did myself in *Moses the Egyptian*: as the proclamation of the One God who, on the basis of the Mosaic distinction, posits his religion as the truth and consigns all other religions to the darkness of falsehood. Neither of the two images does full justice to the Hebrew Bible, but both are contained within it.

This dualism inherent in the Hebrew Bible, this Janus face, has not just caught the attention of theologians. A particularly striking example is Sigmund Freud's book on Moses, which I discuss in more detail in chapter 4. Freud distinguishes between two Moses figures, an "Egyptian" and a "Midianite Moses." One stands for a sublime monotheism, for what is referred to here as "counterreligion," the modern stratum of the Hebrew Bible. The other is considered by Freud to have been a follower of the volcanic god Yahweh and the representative of a typical tribal religion; he therefore stands for the archaic stratum of the Bible.

Far from resulting from the shift to monotheism, the Bible thus still reflects in large measure a pre-monotheistic religious form. Yet monotheism can already be discerned in the Bible as a general tendency. The texts compiled therein straddle this divide, bearing witness as much to the polytheistic point of departure as to the monotheistic end-state, and in particular to the conflicts that arose in the transition from one to the other. For the monotheistic religion by no means followed upon the archaic religion as the logical next stage in its development; the relationship between monotheistic and archaic religions is one of revolution, not evolution. My argument, then, is that the monotheistic shift, which lies between the two images combined in the biblical writings as in a picture puzzle and organizes their differences, takes the form of a rupture, a break with the past that rests on the distinction between truth and falsehood and generates, over the subsequent course of its reception, the distinction between Jews and Gentiles, Christians and pagans, Christians and Jews, Muslims and infidels, true believers and heretics, manifesting itself in countless acts of violence and bloodshed. A number of highly significant and central passages of the Old Testament already tell of such violence and bloodshed. This aspect is examined in more detail below.

Having lived for hundreds and thousands of years on the terrain of secondary religious experience and in the spiritual space created by the Mosaic distinction, we Jews, Christians, and Muslims (to speak only of the monotheistic world) assume this distinction to be the natural, normal, and universal form of religion. We tend to identify it unthinkingly with religion as such, and then project it onto all the alien and earlier cultures that knew nothing of the distinction between true and false religion. Measured against this concept of religion, the primary religions cannot fail to be found wanting: orthodoxy is unknown to them, they barely differentiate themselves from other cultural fields, and in many cases it remains unclear where exactly the boundary lines between divine and natural phenomena, charismatic teachers and normative principles are to be drawn. In these and many other respects, they are not yet "proper" religions. Against the background of this implicit and deeply rooted conviction (naturally, it is not a question of an explicitly formulated theory of religion), a concept such as "counterreligion" is bound to cause offense. What? The highest, purest, and most advanced form in which religion can appear to us, monotheism, is to be called not "religion" but "counterreligion"? How absurd!

What Is Truth?

I want to make clear how this term is to be understood with reference to the parallel case of science. Just as monotheistic religion rests on the Mosaic distinction, so science rests on the "Parmenidean" distinction.[3] One distinguishes between true and false religion, the other between true and false cognition. This distinction, articulated in the principles of identity, noncontradiction, and the excluded middle (*tertium non datur*), is commonly associated with the name of Parmenides, who lived in the sixth century BCE. Werner Jäger rightly speaks of a "constraint on thinking" or cognitive straitjacket that is introduced here: "As he [Parmenides] repeats again and again, with increasing force, Being is, and Notbeing is not. That which is cannot not be; that which is not cannot be—thus Parmenides expresses the constraint on thinking that was established by his realization that a logical contradiction cannot be resolved."[4] In drawing a line between "wild thought"—the traditional, mythic modes of world production—and logical thought, which submits to the principle of noncontradiction, this constraint on thinking places cognition, validation, and knowledge on an entirely new footing. The new concept of knowledge introduced by the Greeks is no less revolutionary in nature than the new concept of religion introduced by the Jews and represented by the name of Moses. Both concepts are characterized by an unprecedented drive to differentiation, negation, and exclusion. Ever since there has been science, and with it a knowledge, based on the distinction between true and false cognition, that distinguishes itself from error and opens itself to criticism through its manner of reasoning, there have also been such distinctions as those between *muthos* and *logos*, wisdom and knowledge, which correspond precisely to the distinction between pagan idolatry and religion. Scientific knowledge is "counterknowledge" because it knows what is incompatible with its propositions. Only "counterknowledge" develops a regulatory code that establishes what is to count as knowledge and what not, that is, a second-order knowledge.

That is why the concept of an ancient Egyptian or Babylonian "science" is to a certain extent anachronistic: in the ancient Egyptian and Babylonian worlds, "knowledge" meant something quite different from what it did for the Greeks after Parmenides. Such concepts nonetheless do their job tolerably well. We all know that the Greeks revolutionized the world by introducing a new, critical concept of truth, and we accordingly take references to a pre-Hellenic "science" with a pinch of salt. As far as religion is concerned, however, this consciousness is nowhere near so well established. Few would suspect that books about Egyptian or Babylonian "religion" use the word in a more or less metaphorical sense. Our concept of religion encompasses both monotheistic and pre-monotheistic religions in an utterly uncritical way. Yet by introducing the Mosaic distinction, the Jews revolutionized the world at least as decisively as the Greeks. They introduced a form of religion that stands out from all traditional so-called religions just as clearly as Greek science stands out from all traditional so-called sciences.

In many discussions in which I have taken part, this thesis has been branded "anti-Semitic." The charge would perhaps be justified had I interpreted this transformation of the world as a turn for the worse rather than for the better, and had I wanted to castigate the Jews for putting an end to a Golden Age of primary religion by introducing the Mosaic distinction. But this strikes me as absurd—no less absurd, in fact, than had I wanted to reproach the Greeks for disenchanting the world and delivering it over to rational calculation through their invention of scientific thought. It is in my view self-evident that in both cases, in scientific thought no less than in monotheism, we are dealing with civilizational achievements of the highest order, and it has never occurred to me to demand that they be abandoned. I am advocating a return neither to myth nor to primary religion. Indeed, I am not advocating anything; my aim is rather to describe and understand. When I characterize scientific thought as counterthought and trace it back to the Parmenidean distinction between truth and lies (or the existent and the nonexistent), it is to draw attention to the potential for negation that inheres in such knowledge, not to criticize and deplore. To put it bluntly, scientific knowledge is "intolerant." The truths of science may well, for the most part, be relative and have a limited life span, but that does not mean that they are compatible with everything else under the sun, for they have their own criteria of validity, verifiability, and falsifiability, which they are obliged to meet. This has become so self-evident to us that it has become practically inseparable from our concept of knowledge. It is what we mean when we speak of "knowledge," and, with Claude Lévi-Strauss, we label a different kind of knowledge "wild thought" and "bricolage."[5]

The concept of "counterreligion" is intended to draw out the potential for negation that inheres within secondary religions. These religions are also essentially "intolerant," although again, this should not be taken as a reproach. Two hundred and fifty years ago, David Hume not only argued that polytheism is far older than monotheism, he also advanced the related hypothesis that polytheism is tolerant, whereas monotheism is intolerant.[6] This is an age-old argument, which I had no intention of revisiting in my Moses book. Secondary religions *must* be intolerant, that is, they must have a clear conception of what they feel to be incompatible with their truths if these truths are to exert the life-shaping authority, normativity, and binding force that they claim for themselves. In each case, counterreligions have transformed, from the ground up, the historical realities amidst which they appeared. Their critical and transformative force is sustained by their negative energy, their power of negation and exclusion. How they deal with their structural intolerance is another matter. That is not my concern here, although I want to note in passing my belief that religions ought to work through the problem rather than attempting to deny that it even exists. Significant progress has undoubtedly been made on this front in recent years.

Science's intolerance or potential for negation is expressed in two directions: in its capacity to distinguish between nonscientific and scientific knowledge, on the one hand, and between false and correct scientific knowledge, on the other. Myths are forms of nonscientific knowledge, but they are not for that reason erroneous. Scientific errors are instances of disproved scientific knowledge, but they are not for that reason mythic. We find something similar when we look at counterreligions. Primary religions are "pagan," but they are not for that reason heretical; heresies are heterodox opinions and practices, but they are not for that reason primary religions, nor are they pagan.

The analogy between religion and science, as well as between the Mosaic and Parmenidean—or Socratic, Platonic, and Aristotelian—distinctions, could be spun out much further. But more is at stake here than a mere analogy. The new concept of knowledge has as its corollary that it defines itself against an equally new counterconcept, that of "faith." Faith in this new sense means holding something to be true that, even though I cannot establish its veracity on scientific grounds, nonetheless raises a claim to truth of the highest authority. Knowledge is not identical to faith, since it concerns a truth that is merely relative and refutable, yet nonetheless ascertainable and critically verifiable; faith is not identical to knowledge, since it concerns a truth that is critically nonverifiable, yet nonetheless absolute, irrefutable, and revealed. Prior to this distinction, there existed neither the concept of knowledge that is constitutive for science nor the concept of faith that is constitutive for revealed religion. Knowledge and faith, and therefore science and religion, were one and the same. Book titles like *Der Glaube der Hellenen* (The Faith of the Hellenes) (Ulrich von Wilamowitz-Möllendorff; Berlin, 1931) and *Der Götterglaube im alten Ägypten* (Belief in the Gods in Ancient Egypt) (Hermann Kees; Leipzig, 1941) are basically meaningless, since the gods of primary religions were not objects of faith in the new sense of this counterevidential (*quia absurdum*) holding-to-be-true, but the preserve of a plain and natural evidence banished by monotheism to the realm of idolatry and pagan nature worship. The ancient Egyptians, like all other adherents of primary religions, knew about the gods rather than believing in them, and this knowledge was not defined in terms of "true and false," but allowed statements that, to our eyes, seem to contradict each other to stand side by side.

There are four simple or original kinds of truth: truths of experience (e.g., "all humans are mortal"), mathematical or geometrical truths (e.g., "twice two is four"), historical truths (e.g., "Auschwitz"), and truths conducive to life (e.g., "human rights"). The Mosaic distinction introduces a new kind of truth: absolute, revealed, metaphysical, or fideistic truth. This fifth truth type does not number among the "simple" or original truths; it represents an innovation. The four simple truths, particularly mathematical and historical truth, were at the forefront of the Greek scientific revolution; in monotheistic religion, by contrast, their place is taken by the fifth truth that enters into the world along with it: "Credo in unum Deum."

Intolerance, Violence, and Exclusion

Many critics felt the concept of the Mosaic distinction to be hostile to religion, even anti-Semitic or anti-Christian, because in their view it implies the charge that hatred, intolerance, and exclusion first came into the world with the Mosaic distinction.[7]

Naturally, I do not believe that the world of the primary religions was free from hatred and violence. On the contrary, it was filled with violence and aggression in the most diverse forms, and many of these forms were domesticated, civilized, or even eliminated altogether by the monotheistic religions as they rose to power, since such violence was perceived to be incompatible with the truth they proclaimed. I do not wish to deny this in the least. Yet neither can it be denied that these religions simultaneously brought a new form of hatred into the world: hatred for pagans, heretics, idolaters and their temples, rites, and gods. If we dismiss such considerations as "anti-Semitic," we consent to discursive and intellectual fetters that restrict our historical reflection in a dangerous way. Whoever refuses to account for the path he has taken for fear that the goal at which he has arrived might prove contingent, relative, or perhaps even undesirable when compared with his point of departure, or the options he has rejected along the way, fosters a new form of intolerance. The capacity to historicize and relativize one's own position is the precondition of all true tolerance.

Against the thesis that monotheism reposes on the distinction between true and false religion, my critics maintain that monotheism is the religion not of distinctions but of unity and universalism. It is instead polytheism that draws distinctions. Each people, tribe, and city has its own tutelary deity and finds expression for its differentiated identity in a correspondingly differentiated divine world. Each deity stands for a distinction. Monotheism cancels and revokes all such distinctions. Before the One God, all people are equal. Far from erecting barriers between people, monotheism tears them down. Thus Klaus Koch writes: "Polytheistic gods are essentially particular and regional. Because they are socialized in line with the community that worships them, they are dismissive, if not downright hostile, towards everything impure and foreign. . . . Consequential monotheism, by contrast, presupposes a deity accessible in all places and to all people. This entails an ethics that applies in equal measure to all, provided the monotheistic horizon is not restricted by a closed society of the elect. The more exclusive the deity, the more inclusive for humankind."[8] As Erich Zenger puts it: "Monotheism is universal, not particular, in its address."[9] Hans Zirker stresses that monotheism, at its core, purports "to conceive of reality as a unity and to postulate a universal history for humankind. Monotheism has its primary meaning not in the mere claim that there is only one god rather than many, but in the way it defines the human world, which ought neither to be drawn into the strife of divine powers and the distribution of regional fiefdoms, nor riven in an insurmountable dualism of light and dark, 'good' Being and 'evil' Being, nor definitively pluralized in the self-affirmation of warring peoples."[10] That is a Christian conception. The real distinction that Christianity sets out to revoke is missing from Zirker's list: it is the border between Jews and Gentiles drawn by the law, particularly through the mark of circumcision. Christianity rests on the universalization of the Mosaic distinction, which now applies not just to the Jews but to everyone else as well.[11]

That is why objections of this kind were barely heard from Jewish quarters. Judaism is a culture of difference. For Judaism, it is utterly self-evident that monotheism draws a border and that the Jews are responsible for policing this border. Assimilation is no less abhorrent to Judaism than discrimination is to Christianity. For Jewish readers, the category of the Mosaic distinction is therefore not a problem, but something that goes without saying. In Judaism, the universalism inherent to monotheism is deferred until a messianic end-time; in the world as we know it, the Jews are the guardians of a truth that concerns everyone, but that has been entrusted to them for the time being as to a kind of spiritual avant-garde. For Christians, of course, this end-time dawned some two thousand years ago, putting an end to the need for such distinctions. That is why Christian theology has blinded itself to the exclusionary force of monotheism. Judaism is a religion of self-exclusion. Through its divine election, Israel isolates itself (or is isolated by god) from the circle of peoples. The law erects a high wall around the chosen people, a cordon sanitaire that prevents any contamination by, or assimilation of, the ideas and customs of the environment. This act of self-isolation has no need to resort to violence, or at any rate to persecute those who hold differing beliefs. The massacres recounted in the biblical texts—that of the worshippers of the Golden Calf, or that of the priests of Baal at the command of Elijah and Joshua—are an internal affair of the Jewish people; they are meant to wipe out the Egyptians or Canaanites who dwell "among us," in our midst and in our own hearts;

they are directed inwards, not outwards. The "peoples" (*gojîm*) are free to worship whomsoever and howsoever they wish.[12] Christianity and Islam, by contrast, do not recognize this border, and they have therefore lashed out in violence again and again throughout their history. Whereas the Jewish people's belief in its own election requires that it exclude itself, the Christian obligation to evangelize and the Muslim obligation to compel submission require that they both exclude the Other. In choosing Israel to be his people, god marks it out from all other peoples and forbids it to adopt the customs of the environment. By commanding Christians and Muslims to spread the truth to all four corners of the earth, god ensures that those who close their minds to this truth will be shut out. Only in this form does monotheism's inherent potential for exclusion explode into violence.

These considerations are equally germane to the problem of tolerance. Intolerance stems from an incapacity or unwillingness to tolerate differing opinions and the practices that result from such opinions. This presupposes not just the distinction between what is one's own and what is not, but an incompatibility between the two established through the distinction between truth and falsehood. Tolerance rests on the same presuppositions. I can only "tolerate" something, in the strict sense of the word, that runs counter to my own views, yet which I can afford to tolerate because I am powerful or generous enough not to have to treat it as a threat. It thus makes no sense to talk of "tolerance" with regard to the polytheisms of pagan antiquity, since here the criterion of incompatibility is missing; as far as other peoples' religion is concerned, there is nothing that would need to be "tolerated." That is why I prefer to speak of "translatability" rather than tolerance, by which I allude to the practice, documented since Sumerian times, of translating divine names—first from one language into another, then from one religion into another as well. Other peoples' religions were felt to be basically compatible with one's own. This is not to say that the peoples who felt this way refrained from violence in their dealings with each other, nor that violence first entered into the world with the Mosaic distinction. It simply means that political violence was not theologically sanctioned, at least not in the sense that those who followed a religion considered to be false had to be converted with the sword. When the Assyrians, for example, referred to the god

Assur in justifying the cruel punishment they inflicted on their apostate vassals, they did so not because these renegades persisted in worshipping their own false gods, but because they had become Assur's enemies by breaking the oaths of loyalty they had sworn in his name.[13] Indeed, the very fact that foreigners could be taken under oath presupposed that their religion and gods could be made to harmonize with the Assyrian deities. The practice of translating deities had already become well established in Mesopotamia by the third millennium, facilitated by the diverse forms of communication between individual city-states that developed within this polycentrically organized space. Contracts with other states had to be sealed by oath, and the gods to whom this oath was sworn had to be compatible. Tables of divine equivalences were thus drawn up that eventually correlated up to six different pantheons.[14] This would have been impossible had it been assumed that the gods worshipped by other peoples were false and fictitious. All contracts were concluded in the name of the gods of both contractual parties. Religion functioned as a medium of communication, not elimination and exclusion. The principle of the translatability of divine names helped to overcome the primitive ethnocentrism of the tribal religions, to establish relations between cultures, and to make these cultures more transparent to each other. That these relations sometimes involved violence and bloodshed is another matter altogether.

It is important to note that the principle of the Mosaic distinction blocked such translatability. Under monotheism, the "peoples" are still free to profess their faith in the one true god at the end of time,[15] but the present forms in which they worship the Supreme Being are not recognized as being equally true. Jupiter cannot be translated into Yahweh. On the basis of this distinction, the Jews would have found it impossible to forge a pact with the Assyrians, since the conclusion of the pact under oath would have implied the equivalence and mutual translatability of Assur and Yahweh. The Mosaic distinction therefore has real and far-reaching political consequences, and I think it likely that these played a crucial role in its introduction. For the Jews, Yahweh could not be translated into "Assur," "Amun" or "Zeus." This was something the "pagans" never understood. After thousands of years of translational practice, the belief had arisen that all divine names referred to the same god. Varro (116–27 BCE) thought it unnecessary to distinguish between Jove and Yahweh, "since the names are of no importance so long as the same thing is intended" (nihil inter-esse censens quo nomine nuncupetur, dum eadem res intelligatur).[16] In his pamphlet against the Christians (*Alēthēs logos*), Celsus argued that "it makes no difference whether one calls god the 'Most High' (Hypsistos), or Zeus, or Adonai, or Sabaoth, or Amun, as do the Egyptians, or Papaios, as do the Scythians."[17] It first becomes possible to profess faith in a god when translatability is obstructed. One can profess faith only in a name, not in a "Supreme Being" ultimately identical with all the other gods, if not "with everything that exists."

For the pagan religiosity of late antiquity, the name of god had been voided of meaning: first, because it was conventional, and second, because god, whom the pagans had likewise come to recognize as the One and Only in and behind the welter of names, had no need of a name anyway, since he was One, and a name is only required where one thing is to be distinguished from others (Asclepius §20, an argument adopted for Christianity by Lactantius).[18] For Jews and Christians, on the other hand, the name of god plays a fundamental role that can decide over life and death, even if that name is presumed to be unsayable or hidden. Qiddusch ha-Schem, "sanctify the name," is the term for martyrdom in Judaism, and the Christians pray: "Hallowed be thy name." In doing so, both pro-fess their unconditional belief in this god and no other.

For this form of intolerance, based on a new awareness of incompat-ibility, what matters is not that violence be inflicted but that it be endured. One must be prepared to die for one's faith rather than agree to actions or beliefs known to be incompatible with true religion. What is important is thus not that divergent opinions and deeds are tolerated, but that one refuse to perform "intolerable" actions demanded by others, such as eat-ing the meat of an animal offered in sacrifice to the Roman imperial cult. Most officials of the Roman Empire had little interest in creating martyrs and were prepared to grant all manner of concessions to the overly scrupu-lous, resting satisfied with minimal forms of compliance. Intolerance was far more prevalent among the ranks of their victims, who were inclined to regard the slightest concession on their part as evidence of "assimilation" and as a falling away from god. Only after the Christians had themselves come to power and Christianity was made the state religion of the Roman Empire was negative intolerance transformed into positive intolerance.

Their fastidious refusal to eat the meat of animals sacrificed to pagan deities then became a ban on carrying out such sacrifices.

Once it is realized that the intolerance inherent to monotheism, which flows directly from the Mosaic distinction, initially appears in a passive or martyrological guise—that is, as a refusal to accept a form of religion known to be false, and a concomitant willingness to die rather than yield an inch on this point—then the problem of "monotheism and violence" can be seen to have as much to do with enduring violence as with perpetrating it. The same can be said of hate. To say that hate came into the world with the Mosaic distinction in the form of hatred for the "pagans," who were first recognized as despicable and excluded as such in the light of this distinction, is to tell only half the story. Of far greater importance than hatred for the excluded is the hatred nursed in their hearts by the excluded themselves. In the Babylonian Talmudic treatise Sabbat 89a, the question of the meaning of the word "Sinai" is posed. "Sinai" is so called, the answer goes, because it is the mountain on which hate (*sin'ah*) descended to the peoples of the world.[19] The other peoples are envious of the chosen people who received the Torah on Sinai.[20] Today, this argument meets with the objection that it amounts to holding the victims responsible for their fate. But what else is martyrdom, if not the responsibility of victims for their fate? To be sure, the Jews murdered by the Nazis were not asked whether they professed faith in Judaism. But this should not blind us to the nature of faith, nor prevent us from seeing how inseparably this category is bound up with the Mosaic distinction.

I have already mentioned that the antagonism characteristic of monotheism as a counterreligion, the exclusive and exclusionary negation by which it defines itself—"No other gods!"—is not just directed outwards, but also and especially inwards. Far more worrying than the paganism of others is the falsehood to which one's own co-religionists are forever in danger of succumbing. The conflict between truth and untruth and the shift from primary religion to counterreligion is played out in the Bible itself. Monotheism relates the story of its own establishment as a history of violence punctuated by a series of massacres. I have in mind the massacre following the scene with the Golden Calf (Exod. 32–34), the slaughter of the priests of Baal after the sacrificial contest with Elijah (1 Kings 18), the bloody implementation of the reforms of Josiah (2 Kings 23:1–27), and the forced termination of mixed marriages (Ezra 9:1–4; 10:1–17), to name only a few examples. Since the Enlightenment, these and other passages have been held against biblical religion by its critics as evidence of monotheism's inherent violence and intolerance.[21] It would be foolish and superfluous simply to restate this critique; we have long since learned that these reported atrocities never took place in historical reality and that, at least in the case of Judaism, no pagans were ever subjected to violent persecution. But it seems to me that it would be equally foolish to explain away these passages with the aim of presenting monotheism as the religion of a tolerant universalism that transcends all differences. The fact that monotheism tells the story of its own foundation and consolidation by drawing on all the registers of violence must surely be of some significance. Here, too, a mnemohistorical change of perspective is called for. The question of how monotheism established itself de facto in Israel, whether through evolution or revolution, by means of gradual transformations or violent reprisals, will no longer stand at the center of the investigation. Instead, we must ask how this process is commemorated in the biblical texts themselves. As far as I can see, there is no historical or theoretical advantage to be gained by trying to deny the semantics of violence inscribed in the biblical texts. Monotheism is theoclasm. That is how it perceives itself, that is how it is presented in the biblical texts, and that is how it has been perceived historically. We would be better off reflecting on how to come to terms with this semantics of violence, rather than sweeping it under the carpet in our eagerness to extol monotheism as the religion of a universal brotherly love.

My aim is not to criticize monotheism but to venture a historical analysis of its revolutionary character, its world-transforming novelty. In this context, it is of decisive importance that the consolidation of monotheism is depicted in the monotheistically inspired passages of the Bible in a sequence of massacres. I am speaking here of cultural semantics, not the history of real events. Monotheism, in other words, is aware of its inherent violence and emphasizes the revolutionary shift that its consequential introduction brings about. I am not interested in peddling the cheap and "rather crude" (Zenger) thesis that monotheism is intrinsically and necessarily intolerant, but in demonstrating the power of negation that dwells within it, the antagonistic energy that translates the distinction between true and false and the principle of *tertium non datur* into a sphere where they had previously been neither found nor even suspected: the sphere of the sacred and the divine, the religious sphere. Through this power of negation, monotheism acquires the character of a counterreligion that determines its truth by expelling whatever cannot be reconciled with it. Neither the Egyptian, Mesopotamian, and Canaanite religions, nor the archaic biblical religion itself can be classified in this sense as counterreligions, unlike the new religion, whose contours emerge most clearly in Deuteronomy and in the other books shaped by this tradition.

Constructions of the Other: Religious Satire

The Mosaic distinction refers, as I have already mentioned, to the distinction between true and false religion. My thesis is that this distinction represents a revolutionary innovation in the history of religion. It was unknown to traditional, historically evolved religions and cultures. Here the key differences were those between the sacred and the profane or the pure and the impure. Neglecting an important deity amounted to a far more serious offense than worshipping false gods, the chief concern of secondary religions. In principle, all religions had the same truth-value and it was generally acknowledged that relations of translatability pertained between foreign gods and one's own. The transition from primary to secondary religious experience therefore goes hand in hand with a new construction of identity and alterity that blocks such translatability. In place of what one could call a "hermeneutics of translation," there now appears a "hermeneutics of difference," which assures itself of what is its own by staking its distance from the Other, proceeding in accordance with the principle "Omnis determinatio est negatio."[22]

What interests me here is what is new in this procedure. Every construction of identity inevitably entails a construction of otherness. There is nothing remarkable about that. The closer the ties that bind it from within, the more sharply a group will demarcate itself from the outside world. But that is only half the truth. Means of intercultural understanding are available to compensate for the gap between self and other that must open up if feelings of solidarity are to arise. All cultures elaborate hermeneutics of otherness and techniques of translation alongside their symbols of identity.

The cultural system of polytheism is one such translational technique. By disarticulating the sphere of the numinous into distinct roles and functions, it converts the divine world of a particular group into a format that makes it compatible with the divine worlds of other groups and cultures. Tribal religions are not mutually translatable in this way. In this respect, polytheism represents a major cultural achievement. As alien to each other as the groups may be in other respects, they can still see eye to eye on their gods. A significant change takes place with the Mosaic distinction, since here it is a matter of "counter"-identification, or, in the terminology of Georges Devereux, "antagonistic acculturation."[23] The "pagan" is not simply "the Other," but the product of a polemical construction. As I have already made clear, the Mosaic distinction bears primarily on one's own religion, within which the distinction between truth and falsehood is drawn; it aims to stamp out pagan tendencies within one's own group and culture. But there is a genre in the Bible that is also concerned with the religion of others, one that casts a deliberately uncomprehending glance at the religious practices of others and exposes them to ridicule in the harsh and alienating light of satiric description: the genre of religious satire.[24]

The beginnings of this form are already to be found in the Bible, in Jeremiah 10, Deutero-Isaiah 44, and in several verses of Psalm 115.[25] The Psalm confronts the invisibility of the biblical god with the visibility of pagan images, which are revealed as fictitious, ineffectual and illusionary precisely in their flashy materiality:

Therefore should the heathen say, Where is now their God?
But our God is in the heavens: he hath done whatsoever he hath pleased.
Their idols are silver and gold, the work of men's hands.
They have mouths, but they speak not; eyes have they, but they see not;
They have ears, but they hear not; noses have they, but they smell not;
They have hands, but they handle not; feet have they, but they walk not; neither
   speak they through their throat.   (Ps. 115:2–7)

Here the target is no longer "other gods" who arouse Yahweh's jealousy, but mere "idols" ('*atzavim*), false, fictitious gods created by the pagans themselves in their benighted state. The absurdity of this kind of image-worshipping religion is expressed still more mercilessly in Deutero-Isaiah's satire:

They that make a graven image are all of them vanity; and their delectable things
    shall not profit; and they are their own witnesses; they see not, nor know; that
    they may be ashamed.
Who hath formed a god, or molten a graven image that is profitable for nothing?

. . . .

The smith with the tongs both worketh in the coals, and fashioneth it with
    hammers, and worketh it with the strength of his arms: yea, he is hungry, and
    his strength faileth: he drinketh no water, and is faint.
The carpenter stretcheth out his rule; he marketh it out with a line; he fitteth it
    with planes, and he marketh it out with the compass, and maketh it after the
    figure of a man, according to the beauty of a man; that it may remain in the
    house.
He heweth him down cedars, and taketh the cypress and the oak, which he
    strengtheneth for himself among the trees of the forest: he planteth an ash,
    and the rain doth nourish it.
Then shall it be for a man to burn: for he will take thereof, and warm himself;
    yea, he maketh a god, and worshippeth it; he maketh a graven image, and
    falleth down thereto.
He burneth part thereof in the fire; with part thereof he eateth flesh; he roasteth
    roast, and is satisfied: yea, he warmeth himself, and saith, Aha, I am warm, I
    have seen the fire:
And the residue thereof he maketh a god, even his graven image: he falleth down
    unto it, and worshippeth it, and prayeth unto it, and saith, Deliver me; for
    thou art my god.
They have not known nor understood: for he hath shut their eyes, that they
    cannot see; and their hearts, that they cannot understand.
And none considereth in his heart, neither is there knowledge nor understanding
    to say, I have burned part of it in the fire; yea, also I have baked bread upon
    the coals thereof; I have roasted flesh, and eaten it: and shall I make the
    residue thereof an abomination [*to'ebah*]? shall I fall down to the stock of a
    tree? (Isa. 44:9–19)

    The text uses the ancient Eastern genre of occupational satire to ridi-
cule the activities of idol-worshippers.[26] This genre operates by representing activities specific to certain professions as an otiose and absurd waste of
time, a useless occupation that serves only to weary, pollute, and deform its
practitioners, thereby excluding them from the community and its norma-

tive hierarchy of socially meaningful conduct. The activities of idol-worshippers are absurd because the idols they purport to influence are works of fiction, nonexistent gods, imaginary powers. Satire relies on a technique of alienation. The described activity or modus operandi is alienated to the extent that the particular presuppositions which make it meaningful are consciously disregarded. In this case, scant attention is paid to the fact that a piece of wood can never be worshipped *eo ipso* as a divine image, but must first be consecrated in an elaborate ceremony that brings it into contact with the world of the gods and fits it to become the temporary vessel of a divine spirit. The reduction to its mere materiality of a cultic image that can only "function" as such in the context of a highly complex semiotics[27] is an alienating trick that places all actions performed in relation to it in an absurd light.

Satire on the "folly of idol worship" receives by far its most extensive treatment in the apocryphal Wisdom of Solomon. Here, no fewer than four chapters are devoted to the theme, in the course of which a number of interesting distinctions are made. The text first deals with those who bow down before natural phenomena, worshipping god's works instead of their author:

> But deemed either fire, or wind, or the swift air, or the circle of the stars, or the violent water, or the lights of heaven, to be the gods which govern the world. (Wisd. of Sol. 13:2)

For this, they are

> the less to be blamed: for they peradventure err, seeking God, and desirous to find him.
> For being conversant in his works they search him diligently, and believe their sight: because the things are beautiful that are seen.   (Wisd. of Sol. 13:6–7)

These nature-worshippers, blinded by the natural evidence and beauty of creation, prove incapable of recognizing their creator. But at least they are on the right track, unlike those who place their hope in "dead things." With that, the text has arrived at the idolaters, whom it characterizes using the satiric form already familiar from Isaiah:

> But miserable are they, and in dead things is their hope, who called them gods, which are the works of men's hands, gold and silver, to shew art in, and

resemblances of beasts, or a stone good for nothing, the work of an ancient hand.

Now a carpenter that felleth timber, after he hath sawn down a tree meet for the purpose, and taken off all the bark skilfully around it, and hath wrought it handsomely, and made a vessel thereof fit for the service of man's life;

And after spending the refuse of his work to dress his meat, hath filled himself;

And taking the very refuse among those which served to no use, being a crooked piece of wood, and full of knots, hath carved it diligently, when he had nothing else to do, and formed it by the skill of his understanding, and fashioned it to the image of a man;

Or made it like some wild beast, laying it over with vermilion, and with paint colouring it red, and covering every spot therein;

And when he had made a convenient room for it, set it in a wall, and made it fast with iron:

For he provided for it that it might not fall, knowing that it was unable to help itself; for it is an image, and hath need of help:

Then maketh he prayer for his goods, for his wife and children, and is not ashamed to speak to that which hath no life.

For health he calleth upon that which is weak: for life prayeth to that which is dead: for aid humbly beseecheth that which hath least means to help: and for a good journey he asketh of that which cannot set a foot forward:

And for gaining and getting, and for good success of his hands, asketh ability to do of him, that is most unable to do any thing. (Wisd. of Sol. 13:10–19)

But the text does not stop at ridicule and satire, rising instead to a tremendous malediction:

But that which is made with hands is cursed, as well it, as he that made it: he, because he made it; and it, because, being corruptible, it was called god.

For the ungodly and his ungodliness are both alike hateful unto God.

For that which is made shall be punished together with him that made it.

Therefore even upon the idols of the Gentiles shall there be a visitation: because in the creature of God they are become an abomination, and stumbling-blocks to the souls of men, and a snare to the feet of the unwise.

For the devising of idols was the beginning of spiritual fornication, and the invention of them the corruption of life. (Wisd. of Sol. 14:8–12)

Here, the concept of seduction is introduced with the word "snare." Graven images are not just useless, they also seduce those who worship them to evildoing. As for the useless, fictitious character of the images, the text points out that the cult of images is a secondary, derivative phenomenon: "For neither were they from the beginning, neither shall they be for ever. For by the vain glory of men they entered into the world" (Wisd. of Sol. 14:13–14). This argument is especially interesting, anticipating as it does the discussion of natural and original forms of religion that so preoccupied the seventeenth and eighteenth centuries. The introduction of the cult of images is traced back to two historical sources: the cult of the dead and that of the ruler.

For a father afflicted with untimely mourning, when he hath made an image of his child soon taken away, now honoured him as a god, which was then a dead man, and delivered to those that were under him ceremonies and sacrifices.

Thus in process of time an ungodly custom grown strong was kept as a law, and graven images were worshipped by the commandments of kings.

Whom men could not honour in presence, because they dwelt far off, they took the counterfeit of his visage from far, and made an express image of a king whom they honoured. . . .

And so the multitude, allured by the grace of the work, took him now for a god, which a little before was but honoured as a man.   (Wisd. of Sol. 14:15–20)

This is no longer satire, but a nascent theory of religion whose theses on the origin of images are worthy of serious consideration. According to this theory, the origins of the cult of images are to be found in the cult of the dead and that of the ruler, in sepulchral statuary and political portraiture. At the time when this text was written, the world was full of statues of the Roman emperor. The obeisance paid these statues counted as a test of loyalty for subject peoples, who could continue to observe their own cults, customs and laws so long as they remained true to the Roman Empire. By worshipping images of the emperor, they publicly demonstrated that loyalty. Images arise on the one hand "from below," from the wish of surviving family members to keep in touch with the departed, and on the other hand "from above," from the need for representation perceived by institutions of government—their need, that is, for a visible presence throughout their entire realm.

The real virulence of this critique of religion relates less to the origin of the cult of images than to its consequences. Here the text indulges in the most outlandish claims:

For whilst they slew their children in sacrifices, or used secret ceremonies, or made revellings of strange rites;

They kept neither lives nor marriages any longer undefiled: but either one slew another traitorously, or grieved him by adultery.

So that there reigned in all men without exception blood, manslaughter, theft, and dissimulation, corruption, unfaithfulness, tumults, perjury,

Disquieting of good men, forgetfulness of good turns, defiling of souls, changing of kind, disorder in marriages, adultery, and shameless uncleanness.

For the worshipping of idols not to be named is the beginning, the cause, and the end, of all evil.   (Wisd. of Sol. 14:23–27)

The charge leveled against idolaters has undergone a drastic transformation. The second commandment and the story of the Golden Calf show no interest whatsoever in other peoples' religions. These are neither persecuted nor subjected to ridicule; they do not even appear on the horizon. What is at stake is one's own religion and the correct form in which it should be practiced. Graven images are not to be worshipped, because this would mean bowing down before other gods, and Yahweh, being a jealous god, would not look kindly on such infidelity. Whether or not other peoples choose to worship their gods in graven images is up to them. That is beside the point. Comparative critique of religion is not the topic of the decalogue. The Wisdom of Solomon, however, is a product of the Hellenistic age, written at a time of conflict between *ioudaïsmos* and *hellēnismos*.[28] Now the narrow perspective of yesteryear has expanded to a universalist position that not only rejects false forms of the Jewish religion, but demonizes and denounces all other religions as pagan. Only now is the theme of idolatry treated with the severity of interreligious and intercultural intolerance. The difference between Israel and other peoples is sharpened into the difference between truth and lies, blessing and curse. Only now does the concept of idolatry, in the sense of a universally valid criterion of true religion, first arise. This concept of idolatry stands and falls with exclusive monotheism, which no longer rests content with worshipping Yahweh alone and worshipping no other gods but him, but categorically denies that other gods even exist. It thereby claims that all other religions worship imaginary and self-engendered pseudo-deities, and that through this aberration, they are sinking ever deeper into a morass of evil, mendacity, and crime. With monotheism as a "regulative idea," the core of this critique is that idolatrous religions are completely lacking in ethical orientation.

CHAPTER 2

Monotheism—A Counterreligion to What?

Monotheism Versus Polytheism

Monotheism and polytheism are concepts born of the theological debates and controversies of the seventeenth and eighteenth centuries. As such, they are completely unsuitable for describing ancient religions. There has never been a religion that defined itself with reference to the concept of plurality, one that adopted *polloi theoi* (many gods) as its motto instead of *heis theos* (one god alone). Nor—at least until the theological radicalization of Islam in the thirteenth century, perhaps—has there ever been a religion that preached a strict and unadulterated monotheism without the interposition of intermediary beings or angels. God's oneness is not an invention of monotheism, but the central theme of polytheistic religions as well. This thesis, which we already find defended in the seventeenth century by the English Neoplatonist Ralph Cudworth, for example,[1] can be verified by examining any number of ancient Egyptian hymns.[2] As an instrument for describing and classifying ancient religions, the opposition of unity and plurality is practically worthless. God's oneness is not the salient criterion here but the negation of "other" gods. This negation is a theological rather than religious matter, a question of divine doctrine as it is determined by theologians and then translated, in a more or less consequential and long-lasting fashion, into religious practice.

The distinction between theology and religion bears on the other argument often held against me: that in historical reality, or at least in the Bible, a monotheism of the kind I postulate on the basis of the Mosaic distinction never existed. My critics then usually remind me that, before and outside the Deuteronomical writings, there arose a belief in JHWH that acknowledged, in addition to JHWH, a *parhedros* such as the Ascherat JHWH in Kuntillat Ashrud or the Anat JHW in Elephantine. Alternatively, my attention is drawn to the "heavenly hosts" and angels that are an essential part even of later Jewish belief forms. For Christianity, the doctrine of the Trinity is regularly cited. From these and similar findings, the conclusion is drawn that there has never been a pure monotheism (except perhaps in Islam), and that the Mosaic distinction is therefore a purely theoretical construct. On much the same level lies the argument that the ban on graven images was never strictly enforced, that images were to be found in Israel in both antiquity and late antiquity, and that Christianity itself made a full return to iconography. Hence there cannot be much substance to the idea of a Mosaic distinction.

The Mosaic distinction, as I stressed earlier, does not designate a historical shift but rather—insofar as it was ever actually converted into real-life practice—an event or moment. In all likelihood, the earliest example of such a monotheistic moment was Akhenaten's coup in the Amarna period. Again, it matters little whether we are dealing here with a case of "pure monotheism," given that the king and queen continued to be paid cultic homage alongside the sun god Aton, given, too, that even the sun god's sacred animal, the Mnevis bull, was openly tolerated. Far more important is the fact that the gods and cults of the traditional religion were abolished and persecuted in accordance with the Mosaic distinction. Here, in Egypt of the fourteenth century BCE, the distinction between true and false in matters of religion was made and this distinction—with all its political, cultural, social, and no doubt also psychic consequences—put into practice for the first time. To be sure, the coup did not inaugurate a lasting monotheistic shift. It was destined to remain an isolated monotheistic moment, even if it did leave indelible traces in religious and intellectual history and doubtless represented a major turning-point, albeit in the pantheistic rather than the monotheistic sense. After the monotheistic episode of the Armana period, Egyptian culture did not simply return to its traditional polytheism, but tried to steer a middle path between the new idea of god's oneness and the traditional plurality of gods. The solution to the dilemma was provided by the idea of the One Hidden God, who manifests himself in the plethora of world-immanent gods as his names, symbols, images, limbs, and visible forms.

The Bible reports several "monotheistic moments," which subsequently relapsed into polytheistic or syncretist practice. To say that the thesis of a Mosaic distinction lacks support in religious history, in the sense that a strict monotheism existed neither in ancient Israel nor in early Judaism, is therefore no argument against it. The Mosaic distinction has its place in a theology of the Old Testament but not in a religious history of Israel[3]—not before Joshua at any rate, if we are prepared to grant the Josianic cultic reforms (2 Kings 22–23) a basis in historical fact. The Mosaic distinction cannot be dated; it stands in the texts, but there can be no doubt that it was also translated into historical reality on many occasions, and with varying degrees of violence, after Akhenaten; and eventually, in a process drawn out over many centuries, it brought about a shift that was to transform at least the Western and Islamic worlds.

The concept of a Mosaic distinction thus refers to a spiritual position, not a historical state of affairs. The ban on graven images, like god's oneness, is a theological rather than a religious affair. Any religion will always be capacious enough to accommodate a variety of different positions, and the Bible in particular, both Old and New Testaments, is of a polyphonic richness that can hardly be surpassed. I have in mind one particular voice and one line in a multivocal concert: the voice of what Morton Smith and Bernard Lang call the "Yahweh alone" faction,[4] the position of Deuteronomy and the Deuteronomical school, the voice of Deutero-Isaiah. What interests me is not whether the demands of this faction were ever fully met in historical reality, but that they were raised and written down at all. The argument that there were still images in Israel cannot explain why the ban on graven images appears at so prominent a place in the Bible, while whoever maintains that the book of Exodus is not about idolatry overlooks the story of the Golden Calf.

It is thus possible that monotheism in the strict sense of the term, the exclusive worship of a single god, is a regulative idea ultimately incapable of institutional realization, an imperative proclaimed by individuals like Akhenaten or the biblical prophets and by movements like the "Yahweh alone" faction or the Deuteronomical school. The history of monotheism is the history of monotheistic moments that, propelled by the revolutionary potential of the Mosaic distinction, unleashed a world-changing force, which nonetheless proved unable to establish itself on a permanent basis as an irreversible and irrevocable achievement.

Let me stress once again that the original meaning of this idea is not that there is one god and no other, but that alongside the One True God, there are only false gods, whom it is strictly forbidden to worship. These are two different things. Asserting that there is only one god may be quite compatible with accepting, and even worshipping, other gods, so long as the relationship between god and gods is understood to be one of subordination, not exclusion. Exclusion is the decisive point, not oneness.

Instead of speaking about mono- and polytheisms, it would therefore be more appropriate to refer to exclusive and nonexclusive religions, or, better still, theologies. We are dealing here with theological ideas, not religions. Monotheism, unlike polytheism, is an idea of this kind. It only attained to the dignity of an idea in the modern age. The question is thus not whether the religion of ancient Israel was poly- or monotheistic, but whether the idea of monotheism can be found in the writings of the Old Testament, and whether individuals and groups who advocated this idea in a particular historical situation can be identified in historical reality. The Hebrew Bible is a polyphonous text. For almost every voice there is a countervoice. The Mosaic distinction is the melody sung by a particular voice, not the refrain of a permanently established religion.

That is no less true of a concept like counterreligion, which implies the concepts of monotheism and the Mosaic distinction. Counterreligion is an aggregate state that no religion can sustain in the long run. None of these secondary religions has ever been able to avoid (and perhaps even wanted to avoid) incorporating into itself elements of the very primary religions it proscribes as pagan. Each secondary religion nonetheless bears within it a "counterreligious moment" that can erupt again under the right conditions. Such moments include the reaccentuation of the Mosaic distinction with which the Counter-Reformation reacted to the syncretism of Platonism and Christianity in the Renaissance,[5] the "dialectical theology" developed by Karl Barth in response to the liberal cultural Protestantism of the fin de siècle, with its historicist relativization of Christianity's claim to truth, and in more recent times, albeit in a different way and in entirely different guises, the modern fundamentalisms, which can be understood as reactive formations directed against the modernization, secularization, and "Westernization" of the world.

It is therefore hardly surprising that the earliest known monotheistic movement was destined to remain an episode: the Amarna religion. Here, at their earliest appearance, we encounter the monotheistic idea and theoclastic violence as products of a particular historical constellation. Unable to establish themselves on a permanent footing, they exited the scene almost as abruptly as they entered it. I suspect that the monotheistic idea could not have established itself in any other form than that of a written tradition. The monotheistic idea can only be guaranteed longevity as a textual corpus, not as an institutionalized religion, at least not in absolute strictness, purity, and consequentiality. This form of "institutionalization through the written word" never eventuated in Egypt and was first realized in Israel.

To sum up, whereas "monotheism" is a regulative idea, "polytheism" designates a religious practice that stands opposed to this idea. There has never been a religion that declared its commitment to polytheism as a regulative idea. Polytheism is a concept suitable only for describing monotheism as a counterreligion that polemically distances itself from other religions. While the concept of polytheism may have served historically as a neutral substitute for the unambiguously polemical and vituperative concept of idolatry ("idol worship"), it has inherited the negative connotations of its precursor, since both concepts have precisely the same meaning in an extensional sense.

Akhenaten and Moses: Egyptian and Biblical Monotheism

The Mosaic distinction between true and false religion finds its single most important formative and normative expression in the story of the flight from Egypt, which represents something like the founding myth of monotheism. Egypt stands for the pagan world, the world of primary religions against which monotheism demarcates itself, and which, with the Exodus, it leaves behind it once and for all. The symbolic significance that the biblical report ascribes to ancient Egypt makes the problem interesting

for an Egyptologist. How does monotheism appear in its origins and manifestations when seen from an Egyptian standpoint, that is, from the perspective of a world that preceded its emergence, and from which it literally
set out to distance itself? We can then see, for example, that two quite different paths lead to monotheism, or rather, that two quite different forms
of monotheism can be reached by following separate paths. One, the evolutionary path, leads to an inclusive monotheism, a monotheism that is
nothing other than a mature stage of polytheism. The other, the revolutionary path, leads to an exclusive monotheism, a monotheism that cannot be arrived at through any developmental process but only through a
revolutionary break with all that went before it. The distinction between
true and false religion pertains solely to this exclusive monotheism.

The history of religion in Egypt confronts us with both forms of
monotheism. The religious reforms initiated by King Akhenaten, who
around the middle of the fourteenth century BCE completely broke with
the traditional religion and introduced in its place the cult of a single
sun and light god, must be understood as an exclusive and revolutionary monotheism. The theology of the ensuing Ramesside era, which reintroduced the traditional pantheon while developing the idea of a hidden
Supreme Being who appears in the world refracted in a polytheistic spec-
trum, can be understood as an inclusive and evolutionary monotheism; it
displays close parallels with the late phases of the Mesopotamian, Greek,
and Indian religions.

Old Testament monotheism should likewise be classified as a revolutionary and exclusive monotheism. Its exclusive character is expressed
clearly enough in the first commandment. Nothing could characterize the
biblical god less aptly than the idea that the other gods are nothing but the
colorful refraction in the world of his concealed essence. It is rather more
difficult to determine what exactly makes this religion revolutionary. Here
one must make a clear distinction between the historical development
of religion in Israel, on the one hand, and the semantics of the biblical
texts, on the other. Religious history makes it seem more than doubtful
whether there was ever a monotheistic "coup" to rival Akhenaten's. As I
have already pointed out, the texts nonetheless tell of a string of exceed-
ingly violent operations, at least one of which, the Josianic reform that
radically purged Israel of all traces of a pre-monotheistic religion, bears

the stamp of a monotheistic coup. Regardless of how the monotheism of the Old Testament actually established itself, whether through evolution or revolution, the texts undeniably present this process, in the hindsight of memory, as a revolutionary deed that had to flush out a good deal of false religion in order that the true religion might prevail. These semantics cannot be dismissed as a fiction. Nor is there anything to be gained by simply declaring these texts to be "late" and dating them to post-exilic or even Hellenistic times. For my purposes it is a matter of relative indifference from what point in time, or even if at all, we can speak of a "really existing" revolutionary monotheism in historical reality; what interests me is the fact that the monotheism developed in Old Testament theology considers itself to be revolutionary, and that it spills a great deal of blood overthrowing the older religions it rejects on account of their untruth. Only this revolutionary, exclusive monotheism will concern us here. It alone is based on what I have called the Mosaic distinction, the distinction between true and false religion behind which, in the final instance, stands the distinction between god and the world.[6]

Akhenaten was evidently the first to put this distinction into practice. We are dealing here with history and not with (retro-projective) theology, as in the case of Moses. Akhenaten did not command: "Thou shalt worship no other gods besides the one light- and sun-god Aton." He simply abolished the other gods and did not consider them worth mentioning after that, not even for polemical purposes. Their exclusion took place on a practical rather than on a discursive and theoretical level. That is why we quite justifiably speak of a Mosaic distinction, not "Akhenaten's distinction." The distinction made by Akhenaten never became a fully articulated, codified, and canonic figure of historical remembrance; it became associated as such with the name of Moses instead. We are nonetheless right to impute the Mosaic distinction between true and false religion, as an implicit theology, to Akhenaten's reforms as well. In view of the common ground shared by Akhenaten's monotheism and Moses', the differences that separate them appear all the more striking.

The monotheism of Akhenaten of Armana was a monotheism of knowledge. Behind it stands a new worldview that makes everything that exists, the sum total of all reality, depend on the effects of the sun, which produces light and heat through its rays and time through its motion.

From the discovery that the sun generates time as well as light, Akhenaten concluded that the other gods had no role to play in creating and upholding the universe. They are therefore nonexistent, nothing but lies and deception. That is why he ordered their temples to be shut down, their cults and festivals abolished, their images destroyed, and their names expunged. This is something completely different from the Mosaic project. Moses set out to establish a new political order, not a new cosmology. He spoke the language of law-giving, constitutions, covenants, and contractual obligations. His concern is with a political monotheism, a monotheism that binds people together. Its motto is not: "There are no other gods but me," but rather: "*For you* there are no other gods," that is, you shall *have* no other gods. The difference to Akhenaten is that here, the existence of other gods is recognized. Otherwise the requirement of loyalty would be meaningless. These other gods are not denied, they are expressly *forbidden*. Whoever falls down before them is not simply deluded, but guilty of committing the worst possible sin. The concept of "false" religion thus has a different meaning for Akhenaten than it does for Moses. What Akhenaten takes to be a mistaken worldview is for Moses evidence of disloyalty or, more precisely, a breach of contract. One is a cognitive category, a matter of knowledge, the other a political category, a matter of mutual obligation. Biblical monotheism is political at its core; this core is very clearly visible in the Book of Exodus and in Deuteronomy, but it is extended in Deutero-Isaiah and other relatively late texts into the cognitive and ontological realms, evolving over many centuries into the conviction that there is only one god and that the "pagans" are worshipping nonexistent gods—idols—not "other" gods.

*Mono*theism therefore has a primarily political meaning. One cannot serve two masters. I may enter a covenant with either god or Pharaoh, but not with both at once, just as a tiny state like Judah could not simultaneously forge alliances with Taharqa and Assurbanipal. This either-or was unprecedented in prior religious history. One could be particularly attached to a deity without for that reason attracting the wrath and jealousy of the other gods, just as one could sacrifice to another god without falling out of favor with one's own favorite deity. The jealousy of the biblical god is a political affect, roused by the wrongdoing of a contractual partner rather than the infidelity of a beloved. However frequently conjugal love and adultery may be mentioned in this context, particularly in Hosea, these are metaphors for a political contract. The contract itself, however, is not metaphorical. It is the matter itself, the new form in which religion—the interrelationship between god, humankind, society, and the world—is recast. This new relationship can only be with a single god, hence monotheistic. This is not to say that there are no other gods, only that, having been shut out of the new relationship to god sealed in the covenant, they are consigned to political irrelevance. One should therefore speak more properly of a monoyahwehism, as is clearly expressed in the formula *JHWH echad* in the Shema prayer. Yahweh is unique, the one god to whom Israel binds itself.

Monotheism as Anti-Cosmotheism

We can understand monotheism of the revolutionary, exclusive kind only by understanding the polytheistic religion against which it is pitted. For this monotheism did not evolve organically from polytheism, but broke with it by denouncing it as pagan. Although, as I have already noted, this monotheism claims universal validity by replacing the many polytheistic tribal and national gods of traditional "pagan" religions with the One God who created and upholds the world, bearing equal responsibility for all, it nonetheless lays down a new, far more important border even as it abolishes the many borders drawn by polytheism: the border between true and false religion. What is to count as true can henceforth only be understood from the position declared to be untrue, and this, in the case of both Akhenaten and Moses, is the traditional religion of Egypt.[7] Revolutionary or exclusive monotheism is anti-polytheism. But what does that actually mean?

Even if we do not believe in him, we all have a basic understanding of what the god of a monotheistic religion is. He is the creator of the world, which he guides in its course and maintains in its existence, an invisible, hidden, spiritual god who dwells beyond time and space, the god addressed by Moses in Arnold Schoenberg's opera *Moses and Aaron*:

Unique, eternal, omnipresent,
unperceived and inconceivable God!

That this is not (yet) the god of the Old Testament need not concern us here: Schoenberg's god more closely resembles the modern, enlightened, Protestant as well as Jewish conception of god, a conception that today's readers can project more or less without difficulty back onto ancient monotheism, so allowing themselves to feel at home in the biblical texts. But what the divine world of a polytheistic religion might be—this we cannot even begin to fathom, let alone believe in it. We must first recognize that after over two thousand years of monotheism, such an understanding has been lost to us. This is where Egyptology, which for the past one hundred and eighty years has sought to make us better acquainted with the Egyptian world, can perhaps take us a step further. Its contribution is no more to be understood as a plea for polytheism than as a critique of monotheism. Egyptology is a cultural science, not a theology. It aims to gain knowledge and understanding, and it abstains from making any normative appraisals. The study of Egypt involves retracing the path of cultural development taken by humankind, at least in the West. Reconstructing this path does not mean wanting to retread it in the opposite direction, something I hold to be as impossible as it is undesirable. I think it important, however, to take into account the turnoffs and intersections that punctuate this path, to see which options were rejected in favor of those we selected, and which helped shape us in turn. In my book *Moses the Egyptian*, I tried to show that the Western world has never stopped hankering for Egypt as the epitome of the rejected alternative.

What, then, is distinctive about a world of gods, in contrast to the One God familiar to us from our Occidental tradition? If we think of the world as a parallelogram made up of god, the cosmos, humankind, and society, then we initially notice that this parallelogram is transformed into a triangle as soon as god is replaced by a world of gods. A world of gods does not stand opposed to the world made up of the cosmos, humankind, and society, but endows them with meaning as a structuring and ordering principle. First, a world of gods constitutes the cosmos, understood as a synergetic process of converging and conflicting forces. For Egypt, at least, it may be said that the cosmos is not so much a well-regulated space as a successful process that results each day anew from the combined actions of the gods. With that, it becomes clear that and how the principle of plurality is ineradicably inscribed into this worldview. The cosmic process would forfeit its synergetic character were it to be understood as the master plan of a single god. Second, a world of gods constitutes society and the state insofar as the gods exercise dominion over worldly affairs. All the great deities are gods of their respective cities; every important settlement stands under the aegis of a deity. The cult is nothing other than the tribute owed the gods as civic overlords. In the political-cultic dimension, the divine world therefore determines the political structure of society, the allegiance of every member of that society to a civic, festive, and cultic community, and the relationship of settlements to cities, cities to provinces, and provinces to the royal capital. In this way, it defines the political identity of the land and all its subdivisions, right down to the individual citizen. Here, too, we see the importance and indispensable necessity of the principle of plurality. This richly patterned sociopolitical identity would blur into a featureless mass were its many gods to be superseded by a single god. Third, and perhaps most difficult for us to comprehend today, a world of gods constitutes the world of human destiny, which in its joys and sorrows, its crises and resolutions, its epochs and transitions, presents itself as a meaningful whole only in relation to the destinies of the gods, that is, in relation to myth. By telling stories about the gods, myths bring order to human life. This meaning-endowing, foundational function likewise stands and falls with the principle of plurality. The gods act out their fate only in relation to each other. A world of gods therefore takes shape as a cosmic, political, and mythic theology, and it is as a narrative about the cosmos, about civic and cultic laws, and about mythic destinies that the divine first becomes word.

That is the theology attacked by monotheism. Plurality is the bone of contention, to be sure, but the decisive factor is not the numerical principle of plurality but the indistinction of the divine and the mundane from which plurality necessarily follows. The divine in the world is inscribed in the three dimensions of nature, state, and myth.[8] Polytheism is cosmotheism. The divine cannot be divorced from the world. Monotheism, however, sets out to do just that. The divine is emancipated from its symbiotic attachment to the cosmos, society, and fate and turns to face the world as a sovereign power. In the same stroke, man is likewise emancipated from his symbiotic relationship with the world and develops, in partnership with the One God, who dwells outside the world yet turned towards it, into an autonomous—or rather theonomous—individual. Therein lies the most significant of monotheism's psychohistorical consequences. This is what "freedom" means in the religious sense. Monotheism transforms the self-image of man no less fundamentally than it does his image of god. That alone suffices to explain why a return to polytheism and to Egypt is out of the question. From where we currently stand in this long history of emancipation and differentiation, we would simply be incapable of it. As Westerners, we cannot live in a spiritual space uncloven by the Mosaic distinction. With the departure from Egypt, an umbilical cord was severed that cannot be reconnected.[9] Through the departure from Egypt, we became free: free from what the Book of Exodus depicts as Pharaonic repression, and free also from a symbiotic relationship to the world that, from the viewpoint of monotheism, appears as a fatal entanglement in the world. At the same time, with the departure from Egypt the divine also emerges from its immanence in the cosmic, cultic, political, and social orders of this world. The Mosaic distinction ultimately signifies the distinction between god and the world, and it thereby establishes the distinction between man and the world.

This cancellation of the symbiotic relationship to the world is what is meant by the concepts of "immersion in the world" [*Weltbeheimatung*] and "negation of the world" [*Nein zur Welt*] used in the German edition of *Moses the Egyptian*,[10] which Erich Zenger professes to finding "barely intelligible."[11] Of course, Zenger is quite right to refer to the "temporal connection and this-worldly orientation" of the Old Testament, and to point out that the "land" is "god's salvational gift par excellence." Gerhard Kaiser and Rolf Rendtorff likewise protest against the charge that monotheism negates the world. That is all perfectly correct, yet it is nonetheless not the same thing as believing in the world's divinity. With the distinction between god and the world, a new distance to the world opens up as well, at least potentially, an inner reserve towards "worldly" goods. Polytheism's total immersion in the world is now relativized. Whoever stands on the ground of the Mosaic distinction does not feel entirely at home in the world any more. Viewed from Egypt, the path taken by Europe presents itself as the cancellation of the symbiotic relationship to god and the world in favor of a transcendent god and a revealed truth. Extreme stations on this path include Gnosticism's radical negation of the world and the Protestant view of the world as a "vale of tears." I am happy to admit that the ancient Israeli religion was not a religion of redemption. But this is not to say that in the writings of the Old Testament, thoughts are not sometimes expressed that would subsequently be developed more fully in the religions of redemption based on those writings. In this sense, we are dealing here, if not with a religion, then at least with a theology—or, to put it still more cautiously, with the germs of a theology—of distantiation, in contrast to religions of complete immersion in the world such as the Egyptian religion.[12]

The opposite of monotheism is not polytheism, nor even idol-worship, but cosmotheism, the religion of an immanent god and a veiled truth that shows and conceals itself in a thousand images that illuminate and complement, rather than logically exclude, one another. We can now get a clearer sense of what the West decided for, and what it decided against, when it opted for Christianity and monotheism; above all, however, we can see that the rejected alternative, the cosmotheism driven out by monotheism, has constantly shadowed the religious and intellectual history of the West, and in certain phases even struck at its heart. Goethe's religion, for example, was cosmotheism, the veiled truth of divine immanence, and he was by no means alone in this. The Renaissance rediscovery of the worldview of antique cosmostheism, along with classical texts and works of art, already had all the impact of a return of the repressed. The figure of Moses the Egyptian stands for this return.

Monotheism as Political Theology:
Ethics, Justice, Freedom

The most important compliment that monotheism has ever paid itself is that it is the religion of justice. According to the widely held conviction of the monotheistic religions, morality and law first came into the world with belief in a single god. "The key point is that ethics gains entry into religion precisely through biblical monotheism (the decalogue)—an entirely novel development, since the gods of Babylon, Assyria or Canaan had nothing to do with ethics in this sense."[13] In this form, the sentence is not entirely false; it first becomes problematic when "entry into religion" is understood to mean "entry into the world," as Hannes Stein, the author of the sentence, intended.[14] First and foremost, monotheism is a great civilizational achievement. Whereas the pagan gods stipulate that their priests be undefiled, their rites correctly performed and their sacrifices plentiful, the god of the Bible is concerned solely or primarily with justice. This god is not served with fatty burnt offerings, but through righteousness and charity. The prophets never tire of emphasizing this point. It is indeed true that one searches in vain for equivalents of such things in Egypt and Mesopotamia. Admittedly, the following extraordinary sentence can be found in an Egyptian text of the Middle Kingdom: "The good deeds of the righteous are sooner accepted than the evildoer's oxen." But the text goes on to say: "Act for god, that he may do the same for you, through sacrifices that richly cover the altar, through inscriptions."[15] In Egypt, one acts for god by making sure that his altars are kept well supplied, and much the same could be said for the rest of the nonbiblical world. In monotheism, by contrast, acting for god means simply "to do justly, and to love mercy, and to walk humbly with thy God" (Mic. 6:6–8). That is why—an objection often raised against the concept of the Mosaic distinction—tracing monotheism back to the distinction between truth and falsehood flies in the face of reality. Truth and falsehood are not at issue here, but justice and injustice, freedom and oppression. Monotheism liberated man to moral responsibility.

This objection is entirely legitimate. Incontestably, the theme of the Book of Exodus is not the distinction between true and false religion, but that between slavery and freedom. In *Moses the Egyptian*, I was not interested in what the theme of the Book of Exodus might be, but in how the opposition of Egypt and Israel developed therein was understood in a mnemohistorical sense, and how it went on to affect the West's traditional image of Egypt. The objection is nonetheless important and warrants a lengthier discussion, which is why I would like to shift my line of inquiry here by treating the biblical text exegetically rather than mnemohistorically. I agree that the distinction between slavery and freedom is central to the Book of Exodus, and we can at least concur that the theme of the book is a distinction. My next step is to argue that the new religion introduced in Exodus is concerned in the first instance with themes like freedom, law, and justice, hence with political theology, and that it alone is defined as the true religion. For the first time in religious history, justice,

law, and freedom are declared to be central themes of religion and the
sole prerogative of god; this is one of the revolutionary innovations of
the Mosaic distinction. The false religion can be recognized by its politics, by the oppression, arbitrariness, lawlessness, and unlawfulness that it
inevitably entails. Monotheism is basically political theology. With that
I am in complete agreement. While it should not be forgotten that the
story of the Golden Calf, likewise contained in the Book of Exodus, deals
with idolatry and not liberation, the ban on graven images also permits a
theological-political interpretation, as will be demonstrated below.

Once the sources are no longer interrogated from a "mnemohistorical" perspective ("how have they been read?"), but with regard to what,
according to the current state of philological research, they mean to say,
one thing becomes clear: the story of the departure from Egypt presents
the emancipatory process set in train by god as an act of political liberation. It is a departure from the house of slavery into freedom. Freedom
may not be a biblical word and it does not appear in this setting, but the
pact with god struck on Sinai is obviously intended as a liberation from
bondage. I see eye to eye with my critics on this, especially with Klaus
Koch and Rolf Rendtorff.[16] But it is another matter altogether to say that
the Mosaic distinction relates exclusively to "free and unfree" rather than
to "true and false." "Free and unfree" bears instead on the content of what
is to count as "true and false." The false religion can be recognized as
such because it subjugates, denigrates, and enslaves. I do not believe that
biblical monotheism can be reduced to law and justice. Of course, Yahweh
flies into a rage at the injustice meted out on the poor, but in the Book
of Exodus what makes him more angry than anything else is the Golden
Calf, notwithstanding the fact that no one was oppressed and exploited
when it was created and worshipped. Everything my critics have to say
about freedom and justice is correct, but it is not everything.

I also agree with my critics in seeing the law as the instrument of liberation from Egyptian and every other form of bondage. Less important
than the act of state-creation is that *the principle of the state be left behind*
and an anti-statist *countersociety* set up in which the influence of the principle of statehood is reduced to a bare minimum.[17] This anti-statist impulse
is staged in the story of the revolt against Egypt. As the epitome of state
authority, Egypt is the house of slavery, not the house of idolatry. False

politics, rather than false religion, is what Israel demarcates itself against when it leaves Egypt and enters into the covenant with Yahweh: the false politics of Pharaonic hubris, repressive rule, enslavement, deprivation of rights, and mistreatment. Whoever feels compelled and constrained by the law is told: "Remember that you were a slave in Egypt." Seen from within, from the viewpoint of the biblical texts, monotheism is originally and primarily a religion of liberation from Egyptian bondage and the basis of an alternative life-form in which, instead of one man ruling over everyone else, people come together in freedom to submit to the authority of a pact they have concluded with god. By being narratively linked to the departure from Egypt, the establishment of monotheism is made to appear as a resistance movement that enjoys divine backing. In the same stroke by which the people is freed from the degrading oppression it had suffered under Pharaoh, the divine or salvation is also emancipated from political representation and becomes the exclusive property of god, who here takes the scepter of historical action in hand for the first time. The story reveals at least a tendency to withdraw salvation from the disposal of temporal powers. From now on, religion and politics are two different things. Great care must be taken in negotiating how they interact, and they can be unified only with violence. I quite agree with Rolf Rendtorff and others when they identify the "political theology" of the Book of Exodus as its chief concern and the question of idolatry as secondary. But that is not how things look from a mnemohistorical perspective. In Hellenism and late antiquity, idolatry shifted ever more to the center of attention as the epitome of false religion, and in the theological controversies of the eighteenth century, it was idolatry, far more than unlawfulness and repression, that was connected with the concept of paganism.

What is perhaps the first case of a violent forced union of political sovereignty and salvation in human history coincides, surprisingly enough, with the first application of the Mosaic distinction between true and false religion. In the entire history of Egypt under the Pharaohs, there is no more extreme case of state-worship than the Armana religion. This is the point in which Akhenaten and Moses, Egyptian and biblical monotheism, prove to be antipodes. The god whom Akhenaten installed in place of the traditional divine world was the sun, a force of nature, a cosmic energy. In that respect, he still remained within the limits of cosmotheism. Only

Akhenaten could enter into a personal relationship with this unmythical, cosmic deity. For his people, this god was simply the sun, from which all life flowed; it did not provide a point of ethical orientation, nor could it be called on to alter the people's fate for good or ill. The king himself stepped into the breach that opened up in this way. He offered himself to the people as the god of an individual and personal piety. Whoever followed him and welcomed him into his heart found salvation, but whoever rejected his teaching could reckon with his wrath:

To those who ignore his teaching he shows his anger,
To those who obey it, his favor.[18]

That was Akhenaten's version of the distinction between true and false, believers and pagans. Akhenaten monopolized the connection between god, humankind, and society, and he thereby restored and considerably reinforced the monopoly on religion that the state had always enjoyed in the form of sacral kingship, but that had been progressively undermined in the New Kingdom, since the fifteenth century BCE, by different ideas about personal piety and the immediacy of the individual's relationship to god. In Akhenaten, the form of Pharaonic hubris and state-worship against which the Exodus myth is directed found its most extreme manifestation.

It is surely no coincidence that the first recorded application of the Mosaic distinction led to a forced union of political power and religious salvation. This points to an ambivalence that inhered in monotheism from the outset. On the one hand, monotheism entails, along with the distinction between truth and falsehood, that between government and salvation. The transcendent god cannot be represented by a profane ruler in the same way as before; as the lord of history, he assumes sole responsibility for realizing salvation. Admittedly, this is not Akhenaten's god, who was neither transcendent nor a god of history, but the sun. Nonetheless, here too the distinction between true and false leads to a radical redefinition of the link between kingship and salvation. The One God receives a royal title, his name is written on cartouches, and he enters as senior partner into a co-regency with the king. The king does not "represent" the absent god on earth as before; rather, both reign together, one as a cosmic, the other as a political and moral power. Here, too, then, the connection between dominion and salvation is strengthened, even as the two are distinguished. But comparable forced unions are also to be found in early Jewish, Christian, and especially Islamic monotheisms, whether in the form of theocracy, Byzantine caesaro-papism, or the usurpation of profane authority by spiritual leaders. Time and again, whenever monotheism ceased being a political resistance movement and established itself as the ruling order, its political theology easily shifted from criticism of the state to legitimation of the state.

If monotheism is regarded from its origins, however, and if these origins are seen from the perspective of the world that preceded them, then it becomes apparent that the political meaning—or the political consequence—of the Mosaic distinction lies in the separation of politics and religion. The indistinguishable, quasi-natural union of kingship and salvation that Akhenaten heightened to an unprecedented degree pertains to the principle of Pharaonic royalty rejected by Moses. As the son of god, the Egyptian king is at the same time the medium of salvation and the embodiment of divine presence in the world. By making salvation the sole prerogative of god and withdrawing it from the control of temporal powers, monotheism ensures that precious little remains of sovereignty apart from a king who must prostrate himself before the Torah and study it day and night. Essentially, royalty disappears; in Judaism, it takes the eschatological form of messianism, while in Christianity, it is invested in the figure of Jesus Christ, whose kingdom is not of this world. Here, too, a symbolic relationship to the world comes to an end, the idea that a divine quality inherent in the world manifests itself in forms of political dominion. This idea has become unacceptable.

Law and Morality in the "Pagan" World and the Theologization of Justice in Monotheism

Like "idolatry," "bondage" belongs to the polemical constructions of the "pagan" on the other side of the Mosaic distinction. Seen from Israel, the Egyptian state presents itself as the "house of bondage"; but how does it appear from the perspective of the Egyptian sources? Surprisingly, the Egyptian state also thinks of itself as an instrument and institution of liberation. There is no word for freedom in Egyptian, just as in the Bible, but the concept of "salvation" approximates what is meant by that term. The state is the champion of "salvational justice."[19] It was set up on earth in order that justice might prevail and the weak be released from their oppression at the hands of the strong. The difference is that in Egypt, the state frees the people from oppression by the natural order, whereas in Israel, the law frees them from oppression by the state.

The king's (and the state's) salvational task of driving unlawfulness from the earth and implementing the law is thematized in a liturgical or "cult-theological" treatise on the king as worshipper of the sun god.[20] The final stanza reads:

Re installed the king
on the earth of the living
for ever and ever,
to give law to the people, to satisfy the gods,
to realize Ma'at [justice], to destroy Isfet [unlawfulness].
He [the king] offers divine sacrifices to the gods
And funerary sacrifices to the dead.

The task of the king on earth accordingly consists in realizing Ma'at and eradicating Isfet. In concrete terms, this means administering the law to the people and making sure that the gods and the dead are kept well-satisfied with sacrifices. The idea of justice is thus accorded a key function in the Egyptian world as well. This justice, however, is not simply restricted to the maintenance of "law and order." We have to distinguish between a "justice from above" and a "justice from below." Justice from above is an organ of the state, put in place to protect rulers from rebellion, property-owners from theft, and order from disturbances of all kinds. The Egyptian idea of Ma'at, by contrast, designates a justice from below, a salvational justice that comes to the aid of the poor and the weak, the proverbial widows and orphans.[21] This justice is not imposed from above, but pushed through from below. According to the Egyptian view of things, it is not an organ of the state. Quite the contrary: the state exists so that justice may be realized on earth.

The Bible is no less concerned with salvational justice, with justice from below. Here it is demanded by the prophets, who speak on behalf of god and in the face of the state. There is nothing comparable to this in the ancient Eastern world, which is why the view that this idea of justice was first brought into the world by the monotheism proclaimed by the prophets could first take hold. In the world of the Ancient Near East, however, there are gnomic texts and mirrors held up to the prince to remind him of the state's mission to institute salvational justice here on earth. The authors of these texts are not prophets speaking in god's name, since they offer only simple, relatively profane principles for regulating individual and community life. In Egypt, the most prominent example is a literary work known as *The Eloquent Peasant.*[22] It tells of an oasis-dweller who journeys to Egypt with his few paltry products in order to exchange them for grain, is robbed on the way, and now seeks redress of his grievances from the local prince and guardian of the law, pleading with him in nine well-constructed, highly poetic speeches to abide by the principles of Ma'at. Its character as justice *from below* could not be indicated any more clearly. The man from the oasis fulfils the same function and registers the same demands as the biblical prophets, but for his own sake and without referring to god.

The monotheistic tradition systematically forgot this prehistory of the biblical idea of justice, insisting that the transformation of reality it effected first brought justice into the world. That is incorrect: justice has been in the world since time immemorial; indeed, it is difficult to see how people could live together without it. But in Egypt, as we have seen, it was situated in the human rather than the divine world. Whereas the gods crave sacrificial offerings, humans crave the law. In its origins, justice is something profane or secular. Religion and ethics have different roots,[23] and in primary religions they constitute separate, albeit interconnected, spheres. Only in monotheism are they fused into an inseparable unity. That this fusion, which represents one of the most remarkable innovations of biblical monotheism, is anything but self-evident has often been underlined from an Egyptological perspective,[24] and it cannot be emphasized enough. Ethics, writes Eberhard Otto, "links up with religion only hesitantly and at a late stage,"[25] while Miriam Lichtheim asserts that "religion and ethics were, and are, two distinct avenues of thought."[26]

What counts as a truism in Egyptology is still the subject of heated debate in other fields of intellectual life. Those who say that, originally and intrinsically, ethics and religion have nothing to do with each other, equally claim that ethics can do without religion. Pierre Bayle unleashed a storm of indignation when he argued as much around 1700.[27] Even

Voltaire contested this thesis, quipping that if god did not exist, he would have to be invented, since nothing else would command respect for the law. But the question is still controversial today, and the thesis that law, morality, and justice are terrestrial and not celestial goods occasionally arouses feelings of deep unease in theological circles. Over the past few years, I myself have twice had the opportunity to air my views on the profane origins of justice before an audience of theologians. The first time they were discussed in a spirit of patience and understanding.[28] On the second occasion, however, in Salzburg in 2000, a man of the church went so far as to claim that my position would logically lead "to abortion, to Sloterdijk's human zoo,[29] and to new Auschwitzes"—such is the bitterness (and blindness) with which, even today, the Church defends the dogma of the inseparable unity of monotheism and justice.[30]

Far from opening the floodgates to godlessness, my thesis that the idea of justice has a secular origin protects biblical monotheism from charges of the kind leveled against it by Friedrich Nietzsche. Nietzsche denounced the principles of salvational justice as "slave morality."[31] He, too, believed them to be an invention of biblical monotheism, which he therefore regarded as the religion of the downtrodden and underprivileged, born of the resentment they felt towards the victorious Greco-Roman culture, which represented the superior values of nobility, wealth, strength, and beauty. No less an eminence than Max Weber vehemently supported him in this.[32] Whoever could show that the biblical principles of salvational justice are also to be found in the wisdom traditions of ancient Near Eastern cultures, and that they formed a widespread basis for regulating the lives of individuals, communities and states, would clear biblical monotheism of this charge, and could further demonstrate that these principles are completely unrelated to resentment and slave morality.[33] On the contrary, we are dealing here with a true master morality, the morality of overlords, conscious of their responsibility towards their underlings, whose sense of their own mastery grows in proportion to their awareness that others stand in need of their protection and patronage. Strength and beauty do not make a master; rather, a person becomes a master by assuming a position of responsibility at the top of a chain of dependence. That is why the Egyptian overlords uphold this morality in their epitaphs, even if they thereby recognize the justice from below demanded by a representative of the underclass in the *Eloquent Peasant* narrative.

Monotheism did not usher law and justice into the world; these had long been in existence. And yet, monotheism's memory is in a certain sense accurate: monotheism may not have invented justice, as is sometimes claimed, but it first made justice a matter of direct interest to god. The world had not previously known a law-giving god. The notion that god is a judge who watches over law and justice, rewarding the just and punishing the unjust, was absolutely central in Mesopotamia and Egypt. In Egypt, justice is a divine idea, but law and the laws are a human institution. They are therefore the prerogative of the king, whose role it is to decree and implement them, and also to suspend them in cases where clemency is granted. In doing so he is not competing with the gods, but representing the divine principle of justice on earth. He still enjoys full sovereignty in his legislative creativity. Precisely this legislative sovereignty is claimed by the biblical god when he appears as a lawgiver. He competes with the king on his own terrain, usurping his position and unseating him from the throne of sovereign, legislative royalty. This type of dominion no longer has a place within the horizon of biblical monotheism.[34]

Monotheism is therefore not without historical justification in crediting itself with having promoted justice and espoused the cause of the law. No "pagan" religion made the law its chief concern. But the monotheistic religion forgot that in the Old World, the state bore responsibility for law and justice, and precisely in the sense of a salvational justice encompassing both law and clemency that characterizes the biblical idea of divine justice. Monotheism's achievement was not to have introduced law and justice, but to have transferred them from the earth and human experience, as the source of the law, to heaven and the divine will.[35] By "theologizing" justice, that is, by placing justice in god's hands, monotheism elevates it to the status of religious truth. Justice becomes the epitome of true religion. With that, lawlessness, immorality, and indecency become attributes of "paganism."

That is why the Bible depicts the pagan religion, not just as idolatrous, but as lawless and indecent as well. Idolatry and immorality go hand in hand. From an Egyptological viewpoint, this is a serious error, if not a willfully malicious calumny. "Pagans and idolaters" such as the

Babylonians and ancient Egyptians had highly advanced moral ideas as well, only for them, these ideas were not anchored in religion, but in other, relatively profane areas of cultural life. Along with the state as the form in which justice came to be institutionalized, "wisdom" needs to be mentioned here as the relevant discursive realm within whose parameters these ideas were developed, codified, and handed down. The ancient Near Eastern wisdom traditions were inherited by the Bible, partly even in the form of translations of whole excerpts, for instance from the Egyptian teaching of Amenemope.[36] The Egyptian expression for this tradition is *sbꜣjj.t*, literally, "instruction, teaching."[37] What these texts set out to teach is not actually wisdom, but good conduct, encompassing table manners and etiquette no less than solemn axioms regulating interpersonal relationships. The pertinent Egyptian word here is Ma'at.[38] Ma'at is a goddess, meaning that we are not moving here in a sphere that is completely unrelated to religion. The sphere of justice is only relatively, not absolutely profane. It is relatively profane because the prescriptions concerning cultic purity, for example, do not number among the moral norms. Here there are no rules like the ban on seething a kid in its mother's milk. The whole area of ritual law, the *caeremonialia* of Thomas Aquinas or *chukkim* of the rabbinical tradition, is missing. Needless to say, there was hardly a shortage of purity laws and taboos in Egypt either, but these were not part of general moral instruction.

Much the same originally held true of Israel. In the Bible we come across exactly the same kind of life rules found in the Egyptian and Mesopotamian wisdom traditions.[39] These life rules do not have the status of *mitsvot*, sacred duties imposed by god himself, but rather that of human guidelines that have stood the test of time, based on traditional knowledge accumulated over countless generations. This relatively profane kind of wisdom is associated in the Bible with the symbolic figure of King Solomon, just as the sacred divine law is associated with Moses. Moses stands for divine law, the form of justice that comes from the alliance with god and hence from the center of the biblical religion, the laws that the people must observe in order to keep their side of the pact with god. In English, German, French, and other languages, these laws tend to be summarized in the singular as "the Law," corresponding to the Hebrew word *torah*. This means something like "instruction," refers to all five books of Moses, and encompasses history together with the law. The bond of history and the law is decisive, since it guarantees the exclusiveness of the law. The law and history are equally holy; they are the laws of god's chosen people, whose justice is founded on them, not on a general ethics.

The profane quality of Solomonic wisdom (*hokhmah*) stands in obvious opposition to this exclusiveness of the Mosaic law. All manner of gnomic sayings found their way into the Book of Proverbs, including one collection translated in its entirety from the Egyptian.[40] The knowledge contained in the anthologies of proverbial wisdom was spread out over the entire eastern Mediterranean. The world-immanent and relatively profane character of Solomonic wisdom contrasts with the exclusive and sacred character of Mosaic law. Here, too, the concept of the profane naturally calls for some qualification. Hokhmah may not be a goddess like the ancient Egyptian Ma'at, but over this entire complex of wisdom stands the sentence: "The fear of the Lord is the beginning of wisdom" (Ps. III:10; cf. Prov. 1:7; Prov. 9:10; Sir. 1:14), and this sentence places wisdom on a religious foundation. In later rabbinical hermeneutics, Torah and Hokhmah come very close to each other and are even conflated at times into a single figure. But we are talking here about origins. And it should be clear that in Israel, the origin of wisdom is as profane and as far removed from cultic practice as in Egypt.

The claim that the "pagan" religions knew nothing of morality is thus untrue in the sense in which it is intended. Morality does not belong to religion in the narrow sense of the term, to cultic sacrifice and its rules of purity. It belongs in the realm of a profane, often corporative or courtly wisdom. It regulates the coexistence of human beings and not their dealings with the divine. My thesis is thus that justice does not spring from the womb of religion, but entered religion from outside. With that, religion is not just ethicized, but above all justice, too, is theologized or sacralized. This process can be observed most clearly from the Egyptian point of view. For the ancient Egyptian texts do not just show us the comparatively profane origins of morality, but its incipient theologization as well.

The Egyptian step towards a theologization of justice lies in the idea that the dead will face judgment, an idea that begins to gain acceptance on the threshold from the third to the second millennium. With this idea, justice is placed on a divine foundation. Even if the monarchy should occasionally fail in its god-given mission to ensure that justice is done on earth, the individual will still have to appear before the gods after his death to answer for how he led his life.[41] The norms that govern the court proceedings, however, are none other than the norms of social life: not killing, stealing, lying, fornicating, insulting the king, despising god, fomenting rebellion, or violating temple property, but also much subtler things like not calling anyone into disrepute before the authorities, not inflicting pain, not letting anyone starve, not making anyone cry, not mistreating animals, not raising the prescribed work rate at the beginning of each day, not cursing and arguing, not eavesdropping, not winking at anyone, not being angry or violent or arrogant, and not turning a deaf ear to words of truth.[42]

The real step towards a theologization of justice in Egypt thus consists not in the involvement of the state but in the idea that the dead will stand trial. Ethical norms are thereby placed on a theological footing. Here, too, however, god appears as judge and not yet as lawgiver. This difference is crucial. For the law by which the god of the Egyptians judges the dead is not divine law but human wisdom. God judges by the same criteria as man. Accordingly, whoever lives in harmony with his fellows also lives in harmony with god. The Bible draws a sharp distinction here, formulating the insight that it is equally possible to suffer for the sake of justice. Only in the context of a religion in which god appears as both lawgiver and judge does the thought first become thinkable that man's judgment and god's can diverge significantly. That is the authentic innovation of biblical monotheism.

Monotheism theologized—it placed in god's hands—preexisting legal and moral traditions, building them at central points into the three-storied edifice of its canon. As god-given instruction, as *Torah*, they enjoy an absolute, atemporal authority. In the books of the prophets, *Nevi'im*, this timeless, god-given instruction is actualized in relation to a given time and interpreted in a historical way. In the *Ketubim*, fine literature, secular wisdom is collected as a form of lived reverence and piety. Only on this level can parallels be found in ancient Eastern cultures. Not even the Codex Hammurabi attained a level of authority in the history of its reception comparable to that of the Ketubim. The Torah and the prophets are unparalleled. The royal decree that proclaims and enacts particular laws is mostly oral; at any rate, it never escapes the constraints of time and circumstance. No sooner has the next king ascended the throne than he makes different laws. Justice is eternal, but the law changes from generation to generation, embodied in monarchs and judicial officials, but not in holy scripture.

By theologizing the law and elevating it to the status of divine law, monotheism freed people from the illusion that without a king to dispense them justice, they would be at one another's throats. With that, the hitherto unquestioned alliance of justice and the state (and of kingship and salvation) comes to an end. This spirit of liberation and autonomy should be preserved with the utmost resoluteness, lest we fall into the erroneous belief that human dignity and human rights would be unable to establish themselves on earth without a judgmental god who is always looking over our shoulders and into our hearts. Humanity will surely never agree upon a common religion. But if religion and the law have different roots, then the hope remains that we will eventually be able to settle on a set of common legal principles. In the debate about what these principles should be, the religions that have espoused the cause of justice will have an important and perhaps even decisive voice, but only in concert with, and without drowning out, all the other, "secular" voices that have devoted themselves to the same cause.

CHAPTER 3

The Clash of Memories: Between
Idolatry and Iconoclasm

The Legend of the Lepers and the
Amarna Trauma in Egypt

One thesis of my book on Moses that came under particularly heavy fire was, put simply, that anti-Semitism was anti-monotheism in its earliest, Egyptian origins. Monotheism, for its part, was originally anti-cosmotheism. It was directed against the divinization of the world, which implies a divinization of mastery. This thesis is based on the assumption of a concealed memory trace in the history of monotheism leading all the way back to Akhenaten, long before the emergence of the Bible's prophetic monotheism. But how are we to make sense of Akhenaten's role in this history without postulating that the Amarna religion exerted either a direct or an indirect influence on the Bible? Many of my critics, pointing out the gulf in time that stretched between Akhenaten and the prophets, as well as the disappearance of any memory of Amarna in the later Egyptian tradition, denied any connection between Amarna and the Bible.[1] But unlike Sigmund Freud, for example, I am not claiming that there is any direct link between Akhenaten and Moses—that is, the beginnings of biblical monotheism. I am not even claiming that somewhere, in Egypt or in Canaan, remnants and recollections of the Amarna religion survived that indirectly affected the development of prophetic monotheism.[2] My thesis is rather that Akhenaten and Moses were *retroactively* interlinked. In my view, a dislocated, legendary memory of the Amarna period was indeed kept alive over the centuries in Egypt, as improbable as this may sound, and was brought into connection with Moses and the Jews in Hellenistic times, when the Egyptians came into contact with Jewish monotheism. The Egyptians reacted with excessive hostility to the monotheism they encountered in the form of the Jews because it came up against an anti-monotheistic predisposition. The sole memory they had retained from the Amarna period, I would argue, was a complex of anxiety and hatred directed towards any form of iconoclasm. This complex found expression in the version of the legend of the lepers told by Manetho. Egyptian anti-Semitism is thus originally anti-monotheism and can be explained from the latent psychohistorical consequences of the Amarna period.

To demonstrate this thesis, I will need to reexamine the "legend of the lepers," which I have already discussed in some detail in the second chapter of *Moses the Egyptian*. Josephus Flavius excerpted it in his pamphlet *Contra Apionem*. In this text, Josephus rebukes the Hellenistic historians of mostly Egyptian descent who recount the Exodus of the Jews in a polemical way that turns the biblical report on its head. Apion himself, against whom, in particular, the work is directed, assumes a prominent place in this anthology of anti-Jewish propaganda. The dossier compiled by Josephus Flavius gives us a surprising insight into the early phase of a pronounced anti-Judaic tendency that is quite clearly concentrated in Egypt. Here, in Ptolemaic and Alexandrine Egypt, a host of central anti-Jewish cliches were coined, which went on to enjoy a long and inglorious career that has lasted up to the present day. The case is important because it shows that hatred for Jews is much older than Christianity, which went on to add several anti-Jewish stereotypes of its own to this sinister repertoire.[3]

The phenomenon of this pre-Christian, specifically Egyptian, anti-Judaism has been adequately noted in the scholarly literature. Two monographs on the theme, from the pens of the Berlin Judaist Peter Schäfer[4] and the Israeli ancient historian Zvi Yavetz,[5] have appeared in recent years. There is widespread agreement that anti-Judaic sentiment flourished in the multicultural climate of Alexandria, where a powerful Jewish diasporic community lived alongside Greeks and Egyptians. Relations between these groups were not always free of tension, leading to strong feelings of animosity, particularly on the side of the Egyptians, who already resented being treated as natives. There is disagreement solely on how the genesis of the conflict is to be explained. Some see in it an initially Egyptian, then broadly pagan reaction to biblical monotheism, whose claim to exclusiveness led it to brand all other religions as idolatrous. Amos Funkenstein, for example, regards these Exodus reports as a "counterhistory," a conscious inversion of biblical historiography designed to destroy the self-image of the Jews by turning their founding narrative on its head.[6] Peter Schäfer, on the other hand, rejects such interpretations as essentialist and insists on the historical contingency of the process. This was not grounded in any "nature of the matter" but can be explained solely through the concatenation of particular historical constellations and events, hence in exclusively historical terms, not with reference to pseudo-entities like the "essence of Judaism" or the Egyptian character. He wants in any case—naturally from the purest and most understandable motives—to avoid making the Jews responsible for the hatred shown them. The Jews themselves saw things differently; they knew that "on Mount Sinai hate came down to the peoples of the world,"[7] and they took up the burden of this hate for love of the Torah. That gave them the certainty that their sufferings were not in vain, and that there was more to them than the blind contingencies of history. This kind of essentialism does not represent an anti-Semitic cliché, but a motif within Judaism used to invest history with meaning.

If my own interpretation is likewise "essentialist," it nonetheless seeks the core of the conflict not in the "essence" of Judaism but in that of Egypt, more precisely, in a chain of traumatic experiences originating in the trauma of the Amarna religion. I would like here once again to defend this interpretation, which draws primarily on the testimony of Manetho. My argument rests on a telling deviation of Manetho's recension from all other versions of the legend. Whereas the other versions all speak of the Jews, Manetho leaves them out of his report. The sole connection consists of a gloss that was obviously interpolated into the narrative at a later date.

Manetho tells of an Egyptian priest by the name of Osarsiph, who at the time of Amenophis III (the father of Akhenaten, whose name was erased from the king-lists) made himself the leader of a group of lepers. The king had interned these lepers in concentration camps and consigned them to forced labor. A prophecy had warned him that the lepers would defile the land and in this way prevent him, King Amenophis, from seeing the gods. Osarsiph negotiated with the king, obtaining his permission to relocate to the old Hyksos capital of Avaris in the eastern delta. There he organized his people into a leper colony and made laws for them. The first was not to worship the gods, the second not to spare any of their sacred animals nor to abstain from other forbidden food. The third proscribed association with outsiders. Finally, we read, Osarsiph took the name "Moyses." This is the gloss by means of which either Manetho himself or his reader Josephus establishes the connection with the Exodus. The suppressed heretical king and the Jewish arch-prophet are thereby conflated into a single figure. In addition, Osarsiph alias Moyses fortified the city, conquered Egypt, and terrorized the country with the utmost brutality for thirteen years. The lepers laid waste to the towns and temples, turned sanctuaries into kitchens, and roasted sacred animals on the spit. Thirteen years roughly corresponds to the settlement period of El-Amarna. The related events take place in the Amarna period. This legend obviously preserves a vague and dislocated memory of the monotheistic episode of the Amarna period, whose theoclastic character it expresses in no uncertain terms.[8]

Manetho illuminates the Mosaic distinction from the other side, from the side of the pagans. The commandment to worship no other gods becomes in his account a ban on worshipping any gods at all. The ban on graven images becomes the commandment to destroy images and slaughter sacred animals. The self-implicating exclusiveness of the law becomes a ban on intercourse with outsiders. Above all, we encounter here for the first time the discourse of illness. From the standpoint of traditional religion, which rests on the distinction between the pure and the impure, the new religion appears as the worst form of impurity, as leprosy. The Church Fathers would adopt such language and apply it to the pagans and idolaters. Eusebius speaks of the "Egyptian sickness," Theodoret of the "Greek sickness." Idolatry is in their eyes a pestilence and above all an addiction, to be stamped out by adhering rigidly to the withdrawal program prescribed by the law. In the language of illness, particularly in the metaphor of addiction, we find articulated an acute awareness of the traumatic aspects of monotheistic religion, with its distinction between truth and falsehood. Above all, we see that Egyptian anti-Semitism is indeed based on a repression, and hence on a collective psychic disturbance. In the encounter with Jewish monotheism, the Egyptians experienced a return of the repressed, to which they reacted by resorting to violent repudiatory mechanisms.

Manetho's report shows us that and how concepts like "trauma," "repression," and "latency" can refer to cultural as well as psychic phenomena. The repression of Akhenaten consisted in the total eradication of all traces of the Amarna period, including the removal of his name from the king-lists, so that it became impossible to identify, date, and localize the traumatic memories of that time. Consequently, these took on ever more vague and legendary features, sinking into a condition of latency. After one or two generations, people no longer knew with whose name they should associate the theocratic revolution. Nonetheless, Akhenaten's name and personality were not entirely suppressed; memory traces survived under the mask of Osarsiph and formed a "crypt" in popular memory, which was eventually to make possible the identification of Akhenaten with Moses.

Josephus's interpretation of the legend of the lepers as a calumnious distortion of the Exodus tale is a classic case of misreading. It warrants our attention not least because it has been perpetuated by all those readers who, like Josephus himself, are unable to decode the legend's allusions to Egyptian history. For Manetho leaves every informed reader in no doubt that he is dealing with an event quite different from the expulsion of the Hyksos, which he reports on elsewhere, and which Josephus had linked to the Exodus of the children of Israel. Manetho dates the episode of the lepers to the time of Amenophis III, a good two hundred years after the Hyksos, since he introduces the wise Amenophis, son of Paapis (i.e., Hapu), as one of his protagonists. Manetho could assume knowledge of this historical figure amongst his readers, for it still enjoyed cultic reverence at the time he was writing. But Josephus no longer picked up this historical reference, which is why he could lump the two reports together. Josephus takes them both—the reliably preserved, carefully transcribed story of the Hyksos and the legendary, orally transmitted tale of the lepers—to be depictions of one and the same event.

Non-Egyptological readers like Amos Funkenstein, Peter Schäfer, and Franz Maciejewski have followed in his footsteps.[9] They overlook the reference to Amenophis III and hence the Amarna period, reading the story of the lepers as a Hellenistic reaction to Alexandrine Judaism. For the Egyptologically informed reader, however, the allusions to the Amarna period are compelling: the dating to Amenophis III, the confinement of the terror to thirteen years, and above all the unambiguously religious characterization of the conflict.[10] What is at stake is not politics but religion, not exploitation and repression but the destruction of Egyptian polytheism, which had its innermost sanctuary, its holy of holies, in the cult of sacred animals. These details fit neither into the Hyksos time nor into Hellenism, but solely into the era to which Manetho dates these events. If one further considers that immediately following the Amarna period, a plague of epidemic proportions ravaged the entire Near East for twenty years,[11] then the references to a sickness—plague or leprosy—to be found in every variant of the legend become comprehensible as well.[12]

The question then naturally arises as to why Manetho speaks of Osarsiph rather than Akhenaten, the son of Amenophis III, and why he depicts this founding of a religion by royal decree, a revolution from above, as a lepers' revolt. I want to explain this distortion of the historical facts as the result of a suppression, the *damnatio memoriae* of Akhenaten. Following the Amarna period, when Egypt returned to the traditional religion prohibited and persecuted by Akhenaten, his name was struck from the king-lists and the traces of his reign were eradicated as thoroughly as possible. These memories could henceforth no longer be placed with any exactness. People no longer knew the name of the leader who had initiated the reforms; they forgot the extremely regrettable complicity of their own monarchy and drew on the semantics of illness to characterize the unnamable heresy as the worst form of impurity known to Egypt (and incidentally to Israel as well): leprosy.[13]

There remains only the problem of how a memory denied a place in official history, expunged from the king-lists, and entirely lacking material support in surviving traces and monuments, could nonetheless have been preserved, albeit in a badly distorted form, for a thousand years, all the way up to the time of Manetho. Three points can be adduced to support this assumption. First, the persecution of the Amarna religion by no means succeeded in destroying all its monuments. The Amarna boundary stelae remained intact, as did the private graves, and who knows what else was brought to light over time in the course of construction works and the like; our current knowledge of the epoch, after all, is based on a quite remarkable abundance of extant documents. What, to Egyptian eyes, must have seemed the enigmatic, undoubtedly repulsive, and perhaps also physically deformed or misshapen strangeness of the figures depicted on monuments like the boundary stelae of Amarna may well have contributed to legends like the tale of the lepers.[14] Second, many effacements of the Amarna period were still visible on older monuments. In speaking here of "suppression," I do not mean that recollections of the period vanished overnight, only to rise up from the depths of the collective unconscious after a millennium, but that they were marginalized and demonized. Third, this legend was presumably associated at an early stage with memories of the Hyksos, and it revised these memories to the same extent that it came to be inscribed in them. The Hyksos were invaders from southern Palestine who in the seventeenth and sixteenth centuries BCE built up an empire from their capital, Avaris in the eastern delta, ruling over lower Egypt and exacting tribute from upper Egypt. The archeological and epigraphic evidence does not speak for a reign of terror and great suffering. Not until two generations after their expulsion did Queen Hatschepsut present them in this light in one of her inscriptions:

I have made strong what was decayed,
and raised up what was dismembered,
(even) from the first time when the Asiatics were in Avaris of the North Land,
(with) roving hordes in the midst of them overthrowing what had been made;
they ruled without Re,
and he acted not by divine command down to my august self,
I being firm established on the thrones of Re.
I was foretold for a (future) epoch of years
as a born conqueror ("she rises and she conquers").[15]

From the Ramesside period, and therefore subsequent to the Amarna experience, comes a story in which the Hyksos Apophis is presented as a monotheist who "worshipped no god and no goddess" besides Seth. Presumably it was not until this point in time, another two or three generations after the Amarna period and under the impression of recent experience, that the memory of the Hyksos took on the character of a religious conflict.[16] A tradition of a religiously conditioned era of enormous suffering was thus established. These memories did not fall into oblivion but continued to be recounted over the following centuries, enriched with new experiences such as the "Syrian conspiracy" at the turn of the nineteenth to the twentieth dynasty,[17] the Assyrian and Persian conquests, and foreign rule, until they finally became fixed on the Jews.

In my view, however, the most important problem here is not so much how a *memory* could have endured over a millennium, but how a *trauma* could have had such sustained and far-reaching consequences. The real problem is not the stability of the memory but the persistence of the traumatization. The experience of the monotheistic revolution, these thirteen short years narrated by Manetho, became so deeply entrenched in the cultural attitudes of the Egyptians that they reacted phobically towards the Jews.

It therefore remains to be explained why this experience was such a traumatic one. After all, no foreign invaders were involved here. The monotheism introduced to Egypt by Akhenaten was the cult of the sun god, whom the Egyptians had always worshipped as the supreme deity, albeit not at the expense of all the other gods. That was, however, Akhenaten's great innovation. Not the introduction of a new god, but the prohibition and persecution of the old gods must have come as a tremendous shock. Here the experiences of our own postcolonial times have opened our eyes to what it means, for a mentality that believes the continued existence of the world to depend upon the regular and correct performance of rites, to have these rites suddenly discontinued, festivals abolished, holy sites desecrated, images destroyed, cults forbidden, priests persecuted, and the entire traditional cosmos of gods and norms denounced as a web of lies and deception, devil's work and idolatry. The Egyptians were probably the first people in history to undergo this experience, in the fourteenth century BCE. I cannot imagine it to have been anything other than traumatic. Let me reiterate that the decisive factor here is not the idea of god's oneness but the idea of false gods, the notion that there can be something like a false religion, the concept of a truth that does not supplement and augment other truths, but places everything else in a relation of untruth to itself. As the first person to strike the distinction between true and false religion, Akhenaten was way ahead of his time and must have appeared to his contemporaries as a heretic, blasphemer, and madman.

Once the real historical background of the legend of the lepers is laid bare through its connection to the Amarna period, the legend appears in a different light. It is no longer the flagrant example of vicious anti-Jewish calumny that Josephus made it out to be. Anti-monotheism, not anti-Judaism, is in play here. The monotheists are presented as atheists and theoclasts, for the hallmark of this new form of religion is not its adoration of a new god but, I repeat, its persecution of the old gods. While the legend may be polemical in the highest degree, it is not reacting against Judaism, which had only forbidden itself the worship of other gods and excluded itself from the peoples without persecuting other gods and excluding other peoples. Rather, it is a reactive formation induced by the massive theoclasm of the Amarna period.

This thesis has been criticized in particular by Franz Maciejewski, who would like to keep Akhenaten out of the mnemohistory of the Mosaic distinction: "the Mosaic distinction should be restricted to where it belongs in letter and in spirit," namely, to Judaism.[18] Behind my suggestion that the mnemohistorical line of the Mosaic distinction should be extended back to Akhenaten, and anti-Semitism traced to an anti-monotheism older than the Jews, he suspects "the bad unenlightened conscience of the post-Auschwitz era," which has a vested interest in "wresting from the Jews their responsibility for having founded the monotheistic religion (and shifting it onto other, Egyptian shoulders), as if the dedication could be misunderstood in the sense of an accusation."[19] But this was precisely the thesis advanced by Sigmund Freud, who was undoubtedly pursuing other interests at the time. Of course I do not wish to deny the Jews their claim to have founded the monotheistic religion. I want only to point out that Akhenaten must be considered the first founder of a monotheistic religion, if we take the negation of other gods to be the criterion for defining monotheism, and that, at the time this new religion was being instituted, monotheistic hatred of the other gods as well as anti-monotheistic hatred of the "criminal of Amarna" (as Akhenaten is called in a Ramessides inscription)[20] were already on show. Maciejewski has since lent his support to my interpretation of the Manetho text as a dislocated memory of Amarna, and has proposed a much bolder way of including Akhenaten in the mnemohistory of monotheism than I myself would venture. He thinks it possible that "the procedure of counterhistory with which Funkenstein reproaches the authors of Hellenistic Exodus narratives is originally expressed in the biblical Exodus narrative itself."[21] According to Maciejewski, the biblical story of Exodus is for its part a counterhistory, written in reaction to the Egyptian legend in which Hyksos and Amarna were fused. "This means that long before Manetho, the memories of Hyksos and Amarna were set in relation to each other in the central mnemohistorical figure of Exodus: as part of Jewish memory. It is thus irrefutably the Jews themselves who saw themselves, in the Egyptian part of their founding myth, as successors to the Hyksos and children of Akhenaten."[22] The biblical Exodus report does indeed show all the signs of a counterhistory, or at any rate a "narrative inversion," at least in relation to the Hyksos. It turns kings into slaves; an expulsion into a ban on emigration; a descent from the Egyptian throne to insignificance into an ascent from oppression to freedom as god's chosen people. Why should not memories of Akhenaten's monotheistic revolution have found their way into this mnemohistory as well, particularly when one considers that Palestine was intensively involved in the events in Egypt, as letters from the Amarna period testify? I do not want to rule out that possibility, but my main concern here is with the distinction between anti-monotheism and anti-Semitism.

Only the original legend, and perhaps also Manetho, should be interpreted as a displaced memory of Amarna filtered through the Hyksos, although it may well be the case that the connection to the Jews was already established by Manetho. Those who came later, picking the story up in the fullness of its different recensions, associated it solely with the Exodus of the Jews, and Josephus is quite right to detect a polemical intention behind their accounts. The existence of an Egyptian anti-Judaism thus cannot be dismissed out of hand. It finds its explanation in what one could call the "Amarna complex" of the Egyptians, their phobic attitude towards every form of iconoclasm, which in the Late Period came to be connected above all with the institution of sacred animals.[23] The critical attitude of the Jews towards the sacred animals and countless divine images of the Egyptians hit a raw nerve. Like the sacred cows in India during the period of English colonial rule, the sacred animals in Egypt became central symbols of national religious identity under Persian and Greek occupation. The legend of the lepers expresses a nightmare scenario that was obviously both widespread and virulent under conditions of foreign rule: that the Egyptian world might one day be brought to a violent end through the slaughter of sacred animals, the destruction of images and the desecration of cults. Much evidence has come down to us of a specifically Egyptian form of apocalyptic narrative that invokes such a scenario. Subsequent events confirmed that the Egyptians knew what they were talking about, for as it turned out, it was neither the Persians nor the Greeks and Romans who delivered the death-blow to their culture, but the Christians and Muslims. Their demise stood in the sign of monotheistic truth, not political violence.

Hate as such did not come into the world with monotheistic truth, but a new kind of hate, the iconoclastic or theoclastic hatred of the monotheists for the old gods, which they declared to be idols, and the anti-monotheistic hatred nursed by those whom the Mosaic distinction excluded and denigrated as pagans. Making this clear does not mean aspiring to return to a world not yet cloven by the Mosaic distinction. It helps us only to understand the conflict better, and to increase our awareness of the many forms in which it resurfaced in the later course of Occidental history. In this regard, the distinction between anti-monotheism and anti-Judaism might prove quite useful.

What I call "anti-monotheism" designates an attitude directed against the Mosaic distinction, that is, against the distinction between true and false religion. Tellingly, this attitude has since antiquity gone hand in hand with a strong insistence on the unity of the divine. The counterposition to monotheism does not claim "God is Many," but rather "God is One and All." It would therefore be misleading to label it polytheism. What is important is not that the divine be manifold, but that the fullness and richness of its innerworldly manifestations not be hemmed in by any dogmatic boundary lines. In essence, the issue here is the godliness of the world. Jewish, Christian, and Muslim monotheisms draw a strict border between god and the world. Precisely this border was opposed by ancient anti-monotheism as iconoclasm, or rather theoclasm. That is why I have proposed to speak here of cosmotheism instead of polytheism.[24]

Iconoclasm and Iconolatry

Regarded from the Egyptian side, the ban on graven images has a double meaning. One aspect of it is political in nature and turns against the state's claim to represent the divine on earth. The gods, according to the Egyptian view, are far-off and hidden. They have withdrawn from the world and made themselves invisible. In lieu of their real presence, however, they have instituted the state, which re-presents them on earth in the form of kings, images, and sacred animals. So long as the state exists, the gods will continue to dwell within their images and maintain inner-worldly symbiosis. The state is thus at the same time a kind of church. Its primary task is to ensure that the world's connection to the gods is not broken off, even under conditions of divine remoteness. Mediacy and representation take the place of their corporeal presence. State and cult, temple, rites, statues, and images can all give presence to the divine and establish indirect contact with it through the power of the symbol.[25] Where once the original, immediate, and symbiotic divine proximity narrated and imagined by myth had stood, there arises a culturally formed space of divine proximity which rests on the possibilities of symbolic mediation and presencing. The state is the institution of this divine proximity. The Pharaoh rules as the representative of the creator god.

In Egypt, the king can deputize for the creator and sun god Re by ensuring that justice is done on earth. In his law-enforcing rulership over his people, the king reproduces god's dominion over the gods, drawing his authority from this relationship of similitude. The king's mastery does not compete with god's; on the contrary, it replicates that mastery and has it as its precondition. Divine sovereignty, however, needs the king and the institutions of state in order to assert itself on earth, and consequently relies on images to represent it in the horizon of the human world. This is the principle of representative political theology: the ruler as the image of god. It is thus hardly surprising that in Egypt, "god's image" is a common royal predicate.[26] In the eyes of biblical monotheism, the falsehood of Pharaonic paganism is revealed precisely in the category of representation, the sphere of kings, images, and sacred animals. That is why images must be prohibited. Therein lies the hitherto largely ignored political meaning of the biblical ban on graven images. In the ban on graven images, the rejection of false politics finds its most drastic expression. In the Near Eastern kingdoms that surrounded Israel, particularly in Egypt, deities likewise appeared as rulers. They ruled as imperial gods over entire states, such as Assur over Assyria, Marduk over Babylon and Amun or Amun-Re over

Egypt, or as civic gods over cities, such as Enlil over Nippur, Ishtar over Uruk, Re over Heliopolis, Amun over Thebes, and Athena over Athens. But these gods ruled indirectly rather than directly and personally. They ruled primarily not over the people but over the other gods. On earth, they were represented in this function of rulership by the king. Precisely such representation is precluded by the political dimension of the ban on graven images. The prohibition of images means first and foremost that god is not to be depicted. Images are incompatible with the real presence claimed by god and secured by the covenant, that is, with the "living" as well as the political form in which the divine turns towards the world. Images are the media through which the divine is magically brought to presence. The living god, however, cannot be conjured into presence; he reveals himself at the time and in the manner of his choosing. Similarly, god has no need of a king to represent him as judge and lawgiver. That is the political meaning of the ban on graven images.

Among other things, the monotheistic ban on graven images also entails the rejection of cosmotheism.[27] Depiction is considered an act of worship. One should avoid depicting the things of this world lest one fall into the trap of worshipping them.[28] That is why humankind ought to rule the world: not in order that it may be exploited, but to resist turning it into an object of veneration.

Along with its political significance, the ban on graven images has a much more general meaning that transcends the political. It is directed against images as such. The catalogue of prohibitions includes

. . . the similitude of any figure, the likeness of male or female,
The likeness of any beast that is on the earth, the likeness of any winged fowl that flieth in the air,
The likeness of any thing that creepeth on the ground, the likeness of any fish that is in the waters beneath the earth:
And lest thou lift up thine eyes unto heaven, and when thou seest the sun, and the moon, and the stars, even all the host of heaven, shouldest be driven to worship them, and serve them, which the Lord thy God hath divided unto all nations under the whole heaven.
But the Lord hath taken you, and brought you forth out of the iron furnace, even out of Egypt, to be unto him a people of inheritance, as ye are this day. (Deut. 4:16–20)

This much more far-reaching meaning of the ban on graven images, which forbids every figural representation, is directed against the symbiotic relationship to the world of cosmotheism; it repudiates images as a form of innerworldly captivity. Man has been placed above creation, not seamlessly integrated into it. He ought not to worship it in consciousness of his frailty and dependence but rule over it freely and independently. Even the *dominium terrae*, the commandment to subdue the earth, juxtaposes the concept of the image with a list of life-forms:

> And God said, Let us make man in our image, after our likeness: and let them have dominion over the fish of the sea, and over the fowl of the air, and over the cattle, and over all the earth, and over every creeping thing that creepeth upon the earth.   (Gen. 1:26)

Similar terms are used in the covenant which god later concludes with Noah:

> . . . Be fruitful, and multiply, and replenish the earth.
> And the fear of you and the dread of you shall be upon every beast of the earth, and upon every fowl of the air, upon all that moveth upon the earth, and upon all the fishes of the sea; into your hand are they delivered.
> Every moving thing that liveth shall be meat for you; even as the green herb have I given you all things.   (Gen. 9:1–3)

In his freedom, independence, and responsibility, man is an image of god. Like the *dominium terrae*, the ban on graven images is intended to withdraw the world from the sphere of the divine, the sphere inaccessible to human control. It is man's duty to take charge of the world in his own right. In doing so, he acknowledges its godlessness, or rather the exclusive divine claim of the extramundane god. Dominion is the opposite of veneration. The same holds true of images. Matter should be controlled and not worshipped. Images ought not to be worshipped because that would mean worshipping the world.

The ban on graven images thus has a double meaning: it destroys the sphere of representation in which the state legitimizes itself (or purports to legitimize itself) as a church, as the earthly presence of the divine; and it disenchants the world, which otherwise casts a spell on man and turns him away from god. Iconoclasm is tantamount to theoclasm: the gods are to be smashed together with the images in which they are worshipped.

We find ourselves here in a world that still had no conception of art and the aesthetic as a sphere of disinterested pleasure. Images are created for the sake of worship, to establish contact between mortals and gods. The polytheistic religions that monotheism rejects and excludes as pagan pay reverence to a divine world, not to the one and only god of monotheism. As I showed above, however, the divine world of paganism does not stand outside and opposed to the "world," understood as the totality of the cosmos, humankind, and society, but is a principle that suffuses it from within, lending it structure, order, and meaning. A divine world therefore articulates itself as a cosmic, political, and mythic theology, and it is as a discourse of the cosmos, of civic and cultic order, and of mythic destiny, that the divine is brought to speech. Once again, we see that behind the Mosaic distinction between true and false in religion, there ultimately stands the distinction between god and the world.

The monotheistic critique of iconolatric religion, which begins in the Bible with Jeremiah 10, Deutero-Isaiah 44, and Psalm 115, continues in Hellenism with four whole chapters of The Wisdom of Solomon, lengthy sections in Philo, *De Decalogo* and *De Legibus Specialibus*, the treatise *Abodah zarah* from the Mishnah, as well as numerous Christian treatises like Tertullian's *De Idololatria* and Theodoret's *Remedy of Greek (= pagan) Sufferings (Hellenikōn pathematn̄ therapeutikē)*. Jews and Christians agree that iconolatric religion is a kind of madness that befalls pagans with uncontrollable force and prevents them from gaining spiritual knowledge of god. The Egyptian legends, by contrast, represent the iconoclasts as lepers. Each side sees the other as "godless." But whereas, for the monotheistic camp, godlessness consists in the worship of false gods, the cosmotheists see in godlessness a refusal to worship the gods as such. For the "pagans," there is no such thing as a false god. All gods have a claim to be venerated, and what is feared most is not that one may have worshipped false gods but that some god or other, perhaps an unknown god, may have been left out of one's oblations. While the Jews are commanded to rid themselves of all images lest they lose contact with their god, the "pagans" must multiply their images and safeguard them as their most treasured possessions if they wish to remain in contact with their gods.

A text already written with an eye to the triumphant rise of Christianity expresses what is at stake in the cult of images: the hermetic treatise *Asclepius*. The text devotes several chapters to divine images. These may be artifacts of human making but they are anything but "dead matter," since they are ascribed the power to establish a connection to the divine powers and make them present on earth for the duration of the ritual. Images are media for the production of divine proximity. They stand in the context of a cult whose goal is to replicate divine events on earth and bring the gods from heaven down to earth. Through this cult and its many images, all Egypt becomes the "temple of the world" in which the gods take up residence—so long as, and insofar as, this incessant activity is not brought to a halt. And yet, the text continues:

there will come a time when it will be seen that in vain have the Egyptians honored the deity with heartfelt piety and assiduous service; and all our holy worship will be found bootless and ineffectual. For the gods will return from earth to heaven; Egypt will be forsaken, and the land which was once the home of religion will be left desolate, bereft of the presence of its deities. This land and religion will be filled with foreigners; not only will men neglect the service of the gods, but, what is harder still, there will be enacted so-called laws by which religion and piety and worship of the gods will be forbidden. . . . O Egypt, Egypt, of thy religion nothing will remain but an empty tale . . . and only the stones will tell of thy piety. And in that day men will be weary of life, and they will cease to think the universe (*mundus*) worthy of reverent wonder and of worship. And so religion, the greatest of all blessings—for there is nothing, nor has been, nor ever shall be, that can be deemed a greater boon—will be threatened with destruction; men will think it a burden, and will come to scorn it. They will no longer love this world around us, this incomparable work of God, this glorious structure which he has built, this sum of good made up of things of many diverse forms, this instrument (*machina*) whereby the will of God operates in that which he has made, ungrudgingly favoring man's welfare, this combination and accumulation of all the manifold things that can call forth the veneration, praise, and love of the beholder. Darkness will be preferred to light, and death will be thought more profitable than life; no one will raise his eyes to heaven; the pious will be deemed insane, and the impious wise; the madman will be thought a brave man, and the wicked will be esteemed as good. . . .

And so the gods will depart from mankind—a grievous departure—and only evil angels will remain, who will mingle with men, and drive the poor wretches by main force into all manner of reckless crime, into wars, and robberies, and frauds, and all things hostile to the nature of the soul. Then will the earth no longer stand unshaken, and the sea will bear no ships; heaven will not support the stars in their orbits, nor will the stars pursue their constant course in heaven; all voices of the gods will of necessity be silenced and dumb; the fruits of the earth will rot; the soil will turn barren, and the very air will sicken in sullen stagnation. After this manner will old age come upon the world. Religion will be no more (*in-religio*); all things will be disordered and awry (*inordinatio*); all concord will disappear (*inrationabilitas*).[29]

"Not only will men neglect the service of the gods, but . . . religion and piety and worship of the gods will be forbidden"—here we have the first commandment of Osarsiph alias Moses. "The pious will be deemed insane"—this corresponds to the biblical satire of the idolaters. The consequence however, in the estimation of those who worship images, is that the gods will withdraw from the earth and the god-forsaken earth will become uninhabitable. Image-worship thus equates to cosmos-worship or cosmotheism. Images and rites make earth resemble heaven and integrate the human world into the cosmic order. Whoever destroys images severs the tie between heaven and earth, cosmos and society, driving the gods from the world and destroying all civil order. War, theft, perfidy, and violence are the result.

The very same thing that the image-worshipping "pagans" fear from the side of the monotheists, however, the latter impute to the idolaters: that they destroy moral orientations and incite violence, dishonesty, and adultery. For the monotheists, being ensnared in images means being ensnared in the world. By worshipping images, the pagans become entangled in what has been made and will come to pass. Distracted by the allurements of creation, they neglect the creator, who is invisible, far from the world and not to be found lurking in any artifact. This split between creator and creation amounted to an inversion and transvaluation of all habitual forms of thought and belief in the ancient world. Far from implying a split between god and the world, creation was seen to ensure their connection. The creator manifested himself in his creation. In Egypt, this intimate connection could even be pushed to the idea that the world is the body of god, which he animates from within. Such ideas were widely received in Hellenistic syncretism, particularly in Stoic, Neoplatonic, and Hermetic cosmotheology.[30] What Christian theology demonized as idolatry (*idololatria*, *avodah zarah*) was ultimately nothing other than ancient cosmotheism. Whoever worships images destroys the connection to the otherworldly god, since he lavishes his piety on an innerworldly object and thereby directs his worship to the created and the perishable. He loses himself in the world and its values, oriented towards the pleasure principle, the law of the stronger and the "survival of the fittest," whereas the monotheist knows all higher orders and norms to issue from the revelation of an otherworldly god. Conversely, "pagan" cosmotheism demonizes exclusive monotheism as atheism, since this religion requires that all other gods be rejected and persecuted. Cosmotheism does not declare Yahweh to be a "false" god who ought not to be worshipped; on the contrary, it promptly admits the god of the Jews into its repertoire of sacred texts and magic formulations. What scandalizes it is the Jews' refusal to pay the homage owed to all the other gods. This refusal, it fears, will lay waste to the world, leaving it to decay as so much dead matter once the gods, whom it regards as innerworldly powers animating the world from within, have been driven out by the iconoclasts. For cosmotheism, the cosmos is the archetype of the norms that co-found the social and political life of humans. That is why, in its eyes, the acosmism of the iconoclasts destroys social harmony. For monotheism, on the other hand, the order that founds human coexistence is not of this world but flows from an extramundane source. Monotheism finds images an abhorrence because they block access to this source and entangle man in the nether regions of worldliness.

In *Moses the Egyptian*, I was concerned with demonstrating that monotheism never succeeded in entirely suppressing the cosmotheistic option. This option found a ready audience time and again in the course of Western religious and intellectual history. Ancient Egypt played a peculiarly central role in this—reason enough for an Egyptologist to be interested in this curious "afterlife" long after the ancient Egyptian texts had fallen silent. The name of Egypt survived above all in Greek and Latin texts, particularly the *Corpus Hermeticum*[31] and the *Hieroglyphs* of Horapollo.[32] In the seventeenth and eighteenth centuries, the idea gained currency that Moses had not received the monotheistic idea through divine revelation, but learned about it from the Egyptian mysteries into which he had been initiated as an Egyptian prince. With that, monotheism and cosmotheism seemed to have been reconciled. Egyptian cosmotheism appeared as a natural religion in whose womb the idea of the oneness of the divine—Isis as Mother Nature—had been preserved. Moses betrayed this mystery to the Hebrews, and thus to all of humankind. It was around this time, too, that the concept of cosmotheism was coined, referring as much to the pagan religion of antiquity as to the contemporary philosophy of Spinoza.

The end of the eighteenth century saw the discovery of India as a spiritual world. Linguists recognized the affinities between Sanskrit, Greek, Latin, and so on, postulating India as the ancestral homeland of the "Indogermanic" peoples on the basis of this linguistic affinity.[33] With that, India inherited Egypt's legacy of representing cosmotheism as the rejected alternative to monotheism. Only now did the Semitic and Indogermanic spheres begin to face each other as two opposing linguistic, ethnic (or "racial"), and spiritual-religious camps; only now, in connection with India, did cosmotheism or anti-monotheism take on anti-Semitic features. Exclusive monotheism now appeared, precisely in its hostility to images, as a typically Semitic religion, the religion of desert nomads. Fundamental ancient Egyptian phobias were revived. Many elements of anti-Semitism are not Christian but pagan or neo-pagan, which is what led Freud to diagnose anti-Semites as "badly christened."[34]

In my opinion, Freud hit the nail on the head with this remark. The cosmotheistic option has never been completely overcome and eradicated, but has resurfaced time and again in various transformations and guises, as hermeticism, Paracelsism, alchemy, Spinozism, freemasonry, Rosicrucianism, theosophy, and so on. In the twentieth century, movements like anthroposophy, Haeckel's Monist League, the Munich cosmicists, and National Socialist neo-paganism, as well as the many different New Age religions, display obvious cosmotheistic tendencies. In relation to one another, these movements are of course completely different, even antagonistic, and should on no account be lumped together. Still, they do all share an element of anti-monotheism. Studying the ancient Egyptian and Hellenistic sources can teach us much about the origins of this conflict, and so help us to dissolve certain anti-Semitic delusions and phobias in the acid bath of historical analysis.

Prisca theologia and the Abolition of the Mosaic Distinction

A clash of memories also broke out in the Early Modern period, although this time it was not fought between monotheists and "pagans" but within monotheism itself. At issue was monotheism's relationship to its own past. Should this past *ante legem* be rejected as pagan, and should the monotheistic declaration of faith on Sinai accordingly be understood as a conversion? Or was this past to be integrated into the history of truth, and Moses regarded as only one of many vessels of truth and revelation in the ancient world, several of whom, including Zoroaster and Hermes Trismegistus, far surpassed him in antiquity? The second option would mean abolishing the Mosaic distinction. In *Moses the Egyptian*, I linked the project of abolishing the Mosaic distinction to eighteenth-century deism. It could be argued against this that Florentine Neoplatonism of the fifteenth and sixteenth centuries, with its conception of a *prisca theologia,* or *philosophia perennis,*[35] already entails such a revocation. In many respects, the eighteenth century reverts to the fifteenth and sixteenth centuries, so that the intervening seventeenth century can be seen, not just as the prelude to a final abolition of the Mosaic distinction (from the viewpoint of the eighteenth century), but equally and conversely (from the viewpoint of the sixteenth century) as the epoch when the distinction was reintroduced with renewed stringency. These objections occurred to me while reading a book that in some ways represents a parallel enterprise to my *Moses the Egyptian*: Michael Stausberg's *Faszination Zarathushtra* (Fascination Zarathustra).[36] In this book, Strausberg draws on the methods of mnemohistorical research to investigate the reception of Zarathustra (or Zoroaster) in European religious history from the fifteenth to the eighteenth centuries, uncovering a quite similar "memory trace" to the one that, beginning with Akhenaten, led me through the Greek sources up to the eighteenth century. Here too, Neoplatonic texts play a crucial role. The Chaldaean Oracles are for Zoroaster what the *Corpus Hermeticum* is for Hermes Trismegistus.

The mnemohistory of Zoroaster in the West begins with Gemistos Plethon (1355/60–1454), who in the fifteenth century fled from Byzantium to Florence to escape the advancing Turks. He may be considered the earliest representative of the doctrine of a *prisca theologia* or *philosophia*.[37] Plethon elevated his own version of Platonism to the rank of a primordial philosophy by tracing Neoplatonic texts such as the Chaldaean Oracles back to Zoroaster and dating the latter, supported by ancient documents (especially Plutarch), to 5,000 years before the Trojan War.[38] He saw himself almost as the founder of a new religion that would sweep away the differences between pagans and Christians by reinstating an original truth common to all peoples.[39] So far as I am aware, Plethon's was the most radical attempt ever made to abolish the Mosaic distinction between true and false religion. His opponents consequently attacked him as a neo-pagan, as *polytheos*.[40] In his speculative audacity, Plethon was destined to remain an isolated case. Although all later positions indirectly built on him, they never ventured beyond the bounds of Christianity, however broadly those bounds may have been defined. It is nonetheless remarkable that the Early Modern critique of the Mosaic distinction begins with a radical break, and that this break with the biblical tradition legitimates itself with recourse to a supposedly much older and original tradition. The new religion propagated by Plethon presents itself as a restoration of the most ancient. This radical point of departure was substantially toned down when later elaborated in the context of the Florentine Renaissance. The line of development here thus moves from radical heterodoxy to orthodoxy, quite in contrast to the seventeenth and eighteenth centuries, when the initial position of the English theologian and Hebrew scholar John Spencer (1630–93), which he still understood to be basically orthodox, came to be superseded by the ever more radically heterodox positions advanced in deist and Masonic circles.

Marsilio Ficino's (1433–99) concept of *prisca theologia* is no longer conceived as a new religion that transcends Christianity but as a primordial religion and primordial philosophy which integrates Platonism, traced back to Zoroaster and Hermes Trismegistus, into Christianity. Ficino is no less concerned than Plethon with rescinding the Mosaic distinction, but he seeks to do so in an expanded Christian sense that understands Christianity to be a primordial religion prepared and announced by all the ancient religions, rather than in a post-Christian, neo-pagan sense. Behind this conception stands a diffusion theory of truth based on biblical genealogy, according to which religious custom originated with Noah before being spread across the face of the earth by Noah's children and grandchildren. Hermes Trismegistus and then Zoroaster appear as the first in a chain of wise men and theologians who preserved and added to the Adamic or Noachidic primal knowledge, while standing outside the biblical tradition.[41] All religious, normative, and cultural traditions (*sapientia*) have a common origin in god and were codified by wise men in primordial times.

Ficino connects the model of *prisca theologia* with a project to renew philosophy as a life-form, a union of wisdom, piety, and practical activity in the sense of the medicinal arts, pastoral care, and philology. The Renaissance ideal of the "magus" who unites all these roles and skills in his own person was modeled on the arch-magi Hermes Trismegistus and Zoroaster.[42] In conflating theologist and doctor, philosopher and natural scientist, into a single figure, this ideal also implies an abolition of the Mosaic distinction, characterized precisely by its exclusion of spiritual matters from the sphere of worldly occupations and competencies.

The case of Count Giovanni Pico della Mirandola (1463–94) is particularly noteworthy in this context due to the complete volte-face made by this author towards the end of his short life. Having at first enthusiastically embraced the model of *prisca theologia*, he subsequently distanced himself from it in his *Disputationes adversus astrologiam divinatricem*, denouncing it as *prisca superstitio*. He thereby anticipated several of the arguments that led to a stricter reinforcement of the Mosaic distinction in the eighteenth century. With that, Pico moved ahead of his time to the same extent that he moved away from his own previous position.

Agostino Steuco (1497/98–1548) consolidated Ficino's model of ancient theology in his conception of a *philosophia perennis*.[43] He too wanted to abolish the distinction between true and false religion, replacing it with the "concord of the wisdom of all peoples with each other and the concord of this wisdom with the teachings of Christianity."[44] Steuco likewise posits a "perfect divine original revelation" passed down by the great wise men, which had been kept alive over the centuries and disseminated amongst the peoples. Yet whereas Ficino had understood the process of diffusion by which a primordial religion had issued and branched off from a common origin in an evolutionary sense,[45] for Steuco this process stands in the sign of depravation. As the tradition deteriorates over time, Christianity, once the undisputed world religion, finds itself confronted with decadent (per)versions of itself flourishing all around it, to be overcome through a return to the common truth. This depravational variant of the diffusion theorem was to become the dominant cultural paradigm of the seventeenth century. Just as Plethon sketched his vision of unity under the immediate impact of the conflicts that had broken out between the Eastern and Western churches and between Christianity and Islam, so Steuco develops his own in response to the irremediable split between Catholicism and Protestantism. In both cases, and in Ficino, Pico, Reuchlin, and others as well, the return to Zoroaster and Hermes, Platonism and Kabbala as supposedly age-old repositories of truth stands in the service of a remarkably irenic model of tolerance. A solution to contemporary discord was sought in the unity of the origin. Confessional conflicts were to be defused by abolishing the Mosaic distinction and returning to pre-Mosaic figures and traditions.

Francesco Patrizi's (1529–97) project of a *Nova de universis philosophia* is inspired by a similar vision of unity. Here too an overcoming of the Mosaic distinction is envisaged, this time in the form of a convergence theory of truth that postulates complete agreement between five different philosophical movements (four "ancient" philosophies and Patrizi's own philosophy), on the one hand, and Catholic teaching, on the other. With Patrizi, the depravation theorem appears as the history of the decline and fall of a primordial language. This primordial language—the language lost after the Tower of Babel was built—functioned according to the principle of "immediate signification" (to borrow a concept of Aleida Assmann's), that is, its signs partook immediately and naturally of the essence of the signified, whereas later languages function according to the principle of mediate signification, that is, they operate by means of a code that conventionally regulates the relationship between sign and signified.[46] The principle of immediate signification was kept alive only in the magic formulae of foreign tongues, the *onomata barbara*, which retained the power to invoke the signified and bring it to presence. Egypt plays a central role in the context of this "search for the perfect language"[47] due to the discussion of hieroglyphs as "natural signs."[48] Since Aristotle was considered to be the main proponent of a semiotic and linguistic theory based on mediate signification, one can understand why Patrizi and others incorporated anti-Aristotelian polemics into their project of a Platonic semiotics based on immediate signification.[49]

The Tightening of the Mosaic Distinction and the Rise of Paganology

Patrizi's work marks the end of the tolerant intellectual climate of the Renaissance: in 1592, it was placed on the Index of Forbidden Books. In the harsher conditions of the Counter-Reformation, there was no longer any place for the *prisca theologia* and the utopian dream of abolishing the Mosaic distinction. The discourse of Hermes Trismegistus and Zoroaster migrated from Italy to more clement northern climes, from a Catholic to a predominantly Protestant setting, and from philosophy—or the utopia of a unity of theology, philosophy, and medicine—to historical, indeed "antiquarian" research. This phase stands in the sign of philological-historical criticism, on the one hand, and an almost phobic rejection of idolatry, on the other. The Chaldaean Oracles, subjected to close critical scrutiny, are revealed to be no less a product of late antiquity than the *Corpus Hermeticum*. Other sources correspondingly gain in importance: inscriptions, the testimony of ancient historians and the Fathers of the Church, travel reports, and so on. For the first time, the tradition associated with Zoroaster now becomes visible in its otherness and ceases to be appropriated as a primordial or embryonic form of the Western tradition. Along with more concerted efforts to draw a line of demarcation that will keep all things foreign at bay, there emerges, paradoxically enough, an entirely new, much more intensive and methodical interest in the extrabiblical world. Even as the "pagans" are once again ostracized and estranged in the seventeenth century, they are studied as never before. This new "paganology" frequently serves to unmask the epigonal, derived character of pagan texts and rituals, as for instance when the relatively recent provenance of the *Corpus Hermeticum* was established by Isaac Casaubon; but it also represents a reaction to the stricter reapplication of the Mosaic distinction and the renewed outbreak of intolerance it brought in its train.

That one nonetheless cannot speak here of religious historiography in the modern sense of the term is indicated by the second focal point, the new enemy of "Zabiism" or "Sabianism."[50] Zoroaster, in particular, becomes the figurehead of this pagan religion, and hence an object of complete anathema. Zabiism is a synonym for idolatry. The concept of the "Sabians," often confused with the Sabaeans (those who dwell in the kingdom of Saba), but not identical with them, is an invention of the great Jewish philosopher Moses Maimonides (1135–1204).[51] Maimonides had attempted to provide a historical justification for Jewish ritual law, which cannot be justified through reason alone, by presenting it as the "normative inversion" of pagan rites (the law prescribes what is strictly forbidden the pagans, and forbids what the pagans undertake as a sacred duty). In search of such rites, Maimonides stumbled across the religion of the Sabians in *Nabataean Agriculture*, a book by the tenth-century author Ibn Wahshiyya.[52] The foremost characteristics of "Sabian" idolatry were worship of the heavenly bodies and astrology. For Maimonides, paganism was not simply an umbrella term for all religions rejected on account of their untruth but a religion in its own right, something that for him went hand in hand with an ethnic identity as a community, people, or nation: the Sabians, the *'ummat Sabi'a*. The most effective way of effacing a memory is to overlay it with a countermemory. As a counterreligion, monotheism could therefore only establish itself by superimposing new rites on the innumerable rites of the Sabians, which were turned on their head in accordance with the rules of normative inversion. In 1625, Stephen Nettles summarized Maimonides' principle of normative inversion as follows:

Moses ben Maimon in More Hanebucim writes that the end for which sacrifices were commanded did tend especially to the rooting out of idolatry: for whereas the Gentiles worshipped beasts, as the Chaldaeans and Aegyptians bullocks and sheep, with reference to the Celestiall Signes, Aries and Taurus, etc., therefore (saith he) God commanded these to be slaine in sacrifice.[53]

Maimonides contended that Jewish ritual law had no rational basis and needed to be explained in historical terms. He saw the historical explanation for ritual law in its function of weaning the Jews away from the idolatrous sacrificial practices of the Sabians, to which they had become completely accustomed. These pagan rites fell into desuetude upon disappearing under a new textual layer of prescriptions. Maimonides' concept of Sabianism, as a world religion that once reigned supreme and had now been obliterated, negatively mirrors the concept of a *prisca theologia*. Whereas the latter rests on an emphatic integration of pagan wisdom, which seeks to abolish the Mosaic distinction in the light of a common truth, the former rests on a no less emphatic rejection of pagan custom, which seeks to reinforce the Mosaic distinction in the light of an exclusive truth that gains acceptance only gradually and by cunningly adapting itself to historical circumstances.

Although the concept of Sabianism is freighted with unambiguously negative connotations, it is at the same time (already for Maimonides) a source of quite irresistible fascination. The new paganology develops under the spell of this fascination: paganism is researched in its own right rather than as a forerunner to Christianity. The seventeenth century is the Golden Age of paganology and thus also the cradle of religious scholarship. The modern reader must disregard the harsh pronouncements on idolatry and the repeated declarations of abhorrence, which to our eyes fundamentally discredit the scientific nature of these studies but were often a necessary disguise, even in a Protestant context, and appreciate instead the unmistakable curiosity that was directed at the "foreign," a term now understood in a far more comprehensive, historical-critical sense than would have been conceivable in the initial phase of reception, within the confines of the *prisca theologia*. Attention was now lavished on the emergence, development, and structural formation of paganism. Unlike in the fifteenth and sixteenth centuries, the Mosaic distinction—the border between truth and lies, Christianity and paganism, monotheism and polytheism (or idolatry)—is rigidly upheld, but only in order that the excluded other may be studied with a prodigious outlay of erudition and critical acumen. Therein lies the interest for the history of science of the books by John Selden (*De diis syris*, 1610), Gerhard Johannes Voss (*De theologia gentili*, 1641), Samuel Bochart (*Geographica sacra*, 1646), Theophile Gale (*The Court of the Gentiles*, 1669–71), and many others. The diffusion theory of the Renaissance, which traced all knowledge back to a common origin and simultaneously discovered in that origin the guarantee for a lost unity, undergoes a decisive modification through this tightening of the Mosaic distinction. The concept of transfer (*translatio, mutatio, imitatio*) now takes the place of tradition, and across the border in both directions at that, either in the sense that the pagans are said to have borrowed biblical knowledge or that the Bible is said to draw on pagan knowledge. The concept of transfer implies the notion of a border and hence the possibility of border-transcending comparison. One of the most important authors in this respect is Pierre Daniel Huet (*Demonstratio evangelica*, 1679). The distinction between true and false religion is drawn here with the utmost polemical rigor. The five books of Moses, whose authenticity and great antiquity are emphatically confirmed by Huet (presumably against Spinoza),[54] are presented as the original codification of divine truth, the pagan religions as their diabolical copy. This work, as scholarly and renowned in its day as it is apologetic, one-sided, and partisan in intent, can certainly not be reclaimed by the history of science as a milestone on the road to religious history. It was countered, however, by John Spencer in his *De legibus Hebraeorum ritualibus et earum rationibus* (1685), a book that turned Huet's theses on their head and thereby showed what alternatives were possible in the seventeenth century. Whereas Huet depicts pagan institutions as plagiarized versions of the Pentateuch, Spencer turns the tables by setting out to demonstrate that the Mosaic ritual laws had their source in (Egyptian) pagan tradition.[55] Even though what we know today about Egypt and the Old Testament suggests that Spencer may have been mistaken in most cases, he was of course quite right to argue for the greater antiquity of the Egyptian religion compared with the biblical religion. Crucially, however, Spencer absolves the concept of transfer (*translatio, mutatio*) from any suspicion of plagiarism or (bad) imitation. In his *Historia veterum persarum* (1700), Thomas Hyde also employs the concept in this value-neutral sense. Here the Bible is once again the donor and paganism the receiving party. But that Zoroaster was a disciple of the prophet Jeremiah and learned much from him speaks, in Hyde's eyes, in favor of his teaching.

With the concept of transfer or translation, the Mosaic distinction is at least relativized. The border may still be drawn, but it is now porous enough to admit the exchange of goods, whether these be contraband or authorized. The orthodox tightening of the Mosaic distinction in Counter-Reformation Europe is cautiously, but continuously and effectively relaxed. The unambiguously polemical concept of idolatry makes way for the more neutral, or at any rate less judgmental and more descriptive, concept of polytheism. The key concept for seventeenth and eighteenth century paganology is "mystery." Pagan religions are interpreted as mystery religions, which already knew the truth but were required to keep it hidden under the veil of the mysteries, accessible only to a few initiates. Moses then revealed it to his people and transformed the distinction between the initiated and the profane into that between Jews and pagans.

CHAPTER 4

Sigmund Freud and Progress in
Intellectuality

Although psychoanalysts, historians, and theologians paid scant attention to Sigmund Freud's book *Moses and Monotheism* when it was first published, it has over the past dozen years or so, more than half a century since its appearance, experienced something of a comeback.[1] There can be no doubt that this comeback is closely linked to the unprecedented interest shown in recent years in the question of Moses and the origins of monotheism, an interest that has spread beyond the discipline of theology to penetrate historical, philosophical, literary, and broadly intellectual circles, even seeping through to the isolated niche of Egyptology, where the topic likewise began to engage me around ten or twelve years ago. After half a century of latency, Freud's provocative arguments have finally begun to cast their spell over the educated public. It almost looks as if the book's theme has become its fate: repression, latency, and the return of the repressed.

The chief merit of this provocative and problematic book is that it drew attention to monotheism as a psychohistorical problem. With the dawning of this religion, Freud contends, there also dawned a new kind of spirituality, a fundamentally new disposition of the soul. Monotheism is characterized—perhaps one should say analyzed—by Freud as a patriarchal religion, with all the psychohistorical consequences that the relationship to the father (in the sense of the Oedipus complex) typically entails. These include defiance of, and submission to, the paternal will, a euphoric sense of having been chosen, feelings of guilt, and fantasies of both inferiority and omnipotence. If, in Freud's view, the Oedipus complex already represents a universal endowment of the human soul, then the patriarchal religion of monotheism signals a decisive and specifically Jewish intensification of that Oedipal predisposition. In monotheism, the suppressed progenitor of the primal horde returns on a quite different plane, as a norm-imposing superfather who demands that his children show him unconditional love, fidelity, and obedience. It is not so much this thesis itself as the psychohistorical twist that Freud gives to the problem of monotheism that is the genuine provocation of his book, a provocation that has only attracted the attention it deserves in recent years.

Freud himself summed up the psychohistorical consequences of monotheism in a single phrase: "progress in intellectuality." By this he meant the extraordinary moral achievements and feats of sublimation that the monotheistic (that is, Jewish) patriarchal religion—with all the Oedipal implications this concept entails—demands of its sons, and to a lesser extent its daughters. In the Freud chapter of my book *Moses the Egyptian*, I misunderstood the connection between the Mosaic distinction and Freud's notion of "progress in intellectuality." I advanced there a view that I no longer believe to be tenable today, especially since reading Richard Bernstein's *Freud and the Legacy of Moses*.[2] My claim was that, in depicting Moses as an Egyptian, Freud was trying to abolish the Mosaic distinction between true and false religion. I could receive this impression because I came to Freud's book on Moses[3] immediately after reading Spencer, Reinhold, and Schiller and while still under their influence. At the time, the book seemed to me to be continuing a particular discourse of the Enlightenment. Yet it made quite a different impression on me when I reread it recently, probably for the third or fourth time in total. I now think that Freud was trying, on the contrary, to present the Mosaic distinction (in the form of the ban on graven images) as a seminal, immensely valuable, and profoundly Jewish achievement, which ought on no account to be relinquished, and that his own psychoanalysis could credit itself precisely with taking this specifically Jewish type of progress a step further.

The Jewish and Greek Options

Jacques Derrida, the French philosopher to whom we owe so many unsettling reflections, once posed the question: "Are we Greeks? Are we Jews? But who, we?"[4] Heinrich Heine had already answered the question in the following way: "All people are either Jews or Hellenes, people with ascetic and iconoclastic instincts who are addicted to intellectualizing, or people of a sunny and realistic temperament who take pride in their own organic growth."[5] This goes to show that the question is far from new. It has been exercising the minds of Europeans since the nineteenth century, when they became aware of their double, antagonistic origin and converted it into the highly stylized rhetorical opposition of "Hellenism and Hebraism."[6]

The question first arose in linguistics, where the discovery of Sanskrit and the Indo-European language group led to the construction of an "Aryan" origin of European culture.[7] This contrast between the "Aryan" and the "Semitic," at first interpreted solely in linguistic terms, quickly became a commonplace of race psychology and cultural typology, spawning an unending proliferation of conventional dualisms and cultural cliches, which still shape our thinking to this day. As a result, Europeans became ever more incapable of grasping the relationship between "Jewishness" and "Greekness" as one of fruitful cooperation rather than implacable antagonism. The particular twist that Heine's answer gives to the question of European origins lies in its generalization of the alternative. It is no longer a question of Aryans versus Semites, but of a much broader opposition involving "all people." We all find ourselves torn between a spiritualizing or intellectualizing tendency that turns us away from the world and a sensuality that turns us towards it. The former tendency has been bequeathed us by the Jews, the latter by the Greeks. Two souls thus dwell within our breast and vie for supremacy, a Jewish and a Greek soul. Ironically, Heine associates (Jewish) spirituality with the concepts of "instinct" and "addiction," reserving the more complimentary notion of "temperament" for the (Greek) counterpole of being-at-home-in-the-world.

Freud took a similar view of things. He too saw the specifically Jewish contribution to human history in the quest for what he calls "progress in intellectuality."[8] This advance corresponds on the level of human psychohistory to what, on the level of individual psychic life, he calls "sublimation," which for him represents the supreme achievement of psychic growth and maturation. Like Heine before him, Freud also writes in this context of an "instinct," although he goes on to dismiss the concept as inappropriate. "For many of us," he asserts, "it may be difficult to abandon the belief that there is an instinct towards perfection at work in human beings, which has brought them to their present high level of intellectual achievement and ethical sublimation," only to continue: "I have no faith, however, in the existence of any such instinct." Far from owing our most impressive cultural achievements to instinct, we have the suppression of instinct to thank for them. "The present development of human beings," Freud writes, "requires, as it seems to me, no different explanation from that of animals. What appears to me in a minority of human individuals as an untiring impulsion towards further perfection can easily be understood as a result of the instinctual repression upon which is based all that is most precious in human civilization."[9] Judaism is the engine of civilizational progress, which, far from being programmed into the instinctual nature of humankind, is deeply inimical to it. The Jews made the decisive step here, and they did so—here Freud is in agreement with Heine—by spurning images. The second commandment marks the crucial epochal threshold in this narrative of progress.

This view of the second commandment likewise has a venerable tradition. Kant regarded the ban on graven images as the epitome of the sublime (towards which every "sublimation process" tends): "Perhaps there is no more sublime passage in the Jewish Book of the Law than the commandment: Thou shalt not make unto thyself any graven image, nor any likeness either of that which is in heaven, or on the earth, or yet under the earth, etc. This commandment alone can explain the enthusiasm that the Jewish people felt in its civilized period for its religion when it compared itself with other peoples, or the pride that Mohammedanism inspired."[10] Freud's remarks on "progress in intellectuality" read like an extended commentary on this statement. Like Kant, Freud is inquiring into the ultimate foundation of both the coercive force that religion exerts on the Jews—Kant's "enthusiasm"—and the pride they take in being god's chosen people. For Freud, monotheistic religion is characterized by "its rejection of magic and mysticism, its invitation to advances in intellectuality, and its encouragement of sublimations." Under monotheism, "the people, enraptured by the possession of the truth, overwhelmed by the consciousness of being chosen, came to have a high opinion of what is intellectual and to lay stress on what is moral."[11]

"Progress in intellectuality" is the heading given by Freud to the third of eight sections in which he summarizes the findings of his last book, *Moses and Monotheism.* Freud not only published this section as an article in its own right,[12] he approved it to be read by his daughter Anna at the International Psychoanalytic Congress in Paris in 1938.[13] This shows how highly he regarded the text. He saw in it a declaration of his allegiance to Judaism, his legacy as a philosopher of culture, and the quintessence of his book on Moses.[14] One would not, therefore, be mistaken in summing up Freud's understanding of Judaism and the Jewish contribution to human history in the following statement: If it is the destiny of humankind to advance in intellectuality, then the Jews are the ones who lead the way.

The Trauma of Monotheism: Analytic Hermeneutics and Mnemohistory

The question that Freud takes as his point of departure bears on the origin of Judaism. He wants to know "how the Jews have come to be what they are and why they have attracted this undying hatred."[15] What I have just called the Oedipal intensification holds true only of Judaism, just as Freud has Judaism rather than Christianity in mind when he speaks of monotheistic religion. The patri-oedipal intensification of Jewish patriarchal religion is the mental precondition for progress in intellectuality.

Freud's answer to the question of how the Jews have come to be who they are is nothing short of astonishing. "The Jew," he claims, is the creation of a single person, "the man Moses." This man created the Jewish people in a twofold sense. By setting it free, legislating for it, and providing it with a religious doctrine, he molded what had previously been an amorphous mass of slaves into a people, in the sense of a politically organized community. But he also brought it into existence in a second, much deeper sense, by shaping its very soul. This far more decisive creation, which first made the Jews "what they are," did not take place during his own lifetime but was accomplished from beyond the grave. An ethno- and psychogenetic process that unfolded over many thousands of years, it belongs in the realm of secret history. The annals of official memory, the biblical texts and other historical sources, have nothing to say about it. Only the "archeological" apparatus of psychoanalysis can reach down to this subterranean realm of collective spiritual life to reveal an origin that has not just withdrawn from conscious memory, but must, according to all the rules of psychoanalytic theory, have been repressed as a profoundly traumatic experience. According to Freud, no other explanation can account for the dynamism with which an idea could captivate the soul of an entire people and "bring it under its spell":

> It is worth specially stressing the fact that each portion which returns from oblivion asserts itself with peculiar force, exercises an incomparably powerful influence on people in the mass, and raises an irresistible claim to truth against which logical objections remain powerless: a kind of *credo quia absurdum* [I believe because it is absurd]. This remarkable feature can only be understood on the pattern of the delusions of psychotics. We have long understood that a portion of forgotten truth lies hidden in delusional ideas, that when this returns it has to put up with distortions and misunderstandings, and that the compulsive conviction which attaches to the delusion arises from this core of truth and spreads out on to the illusions that shroud it. We must grant an ingredient such as this of what may be called *historical* truth to the dogmas of religion as well, which, to be sure, bear the character of psychotic symptoms but which, as group phenomena, escape the curse of isolation.[16]

For Freud, religious tradition weaves a veil of "illusions," "distortions and misunderstandings," which his quasi-archeological method of psychoanalytic labor lifts away to reveal an underlying core of historical truth. Freud is convinced that he has unveiled this origin rather than reconstructed it, much as Pharaoh Akhenaten (whom he held in great esteem) was rediscovered by nineteenth-century archeologists or, in Freud's own day, Pharaoh Tutenkhamen by Howard Carter.

One of Freud's leading topological metaphors is that of depth. This is closely linked to his topology of the psyche, with its tripartite stratification into It (id), I (ego), and Over-I (superego). The It is the depth dimension of the Unconscious. It lies beyond the reach of consciousness and announces itself solely in traces and symptoms. Analysis is the art of investigating these depths. Freud liked to compare his work to the archeologist's, a fascination to which his personal collection of antiquities likewise attests. He had already begun elaborating this methodological comparison in his early study on hysteria from 1896:

Imagine that an explorer arrives in a little-known region where his interest is aroused by an expanse of ruins, with remains of walls, fragments of columns, and tablets with half-effaced and unreadable inscriptions. He may content himself with inspecting what lies exposed to view, with questioning the inhabitants—perhaps semi-barbaric people—who live in the vicinity, about what tradition tells them of the history and meaning of these archaeological remains, and with noting down what they tell him—and he may then proceed on his journey. But he may act differently. He may have brought picks, shovels and spades with him, and he may set the inhabitants to work with these implements. Together with them he may start upon the ruins, clear away the rubbish, and, beginning from the visible remains, uncover what is buried. If his work is crowned with success, the discoveries are self-explanatory: the ruined walls are part of the ramparts of a palace or a treasure-house; the fragments of columns can be filled out into a temple; the numerous inscriptions, which, by good luck, may be bilingual, reveal an alphabet and a language, and, when they have been deciphered and translated, yield undreamed-of information about the events of the remote past, to commemorate which the monuments were built. *Saxa loquuntur!* [17]

Saxa loquuntur, the stones speak; but what they tell the archeologist who delves into the depths is something quite different from the story that the oral tradition of the semi-barbaric natives or the surface finds alone can yield. The truth dug up from below is fundamentally distinct from the message or appearance that lies exposed to view. The principle of Freudian hermeneutics results from this difference. It is a hermeneutics of suspicion (Ricoeur),[18] which sees only distorted and misrepresented traces of a buried truth in the explicit communications of the surface. Freud approaches biblical texts in much the same way. He purports to glimpse through these texts the outlines of a history that has brought about massive upheavals in the souls of those it has affected and has made them what they are today.

Mnemohistory proceeds in the opposite direction. It inquires into symbolic rather than historical truth. It does not dispense with symbols after it has arrived through them at some buried, forgotten, or repressed kernel of truth, but probes symbols for what they have to say. Rather than asking how it actually happened, it asks how and why it was remembered.

Freud's analysis of monotheism as a patriarchal religion—one could perhaps speak here of "patritheism"—rests on two foundations that are inaccessible to all conscious remembrance (and hence to cultural transmission), and that could only be brought to light again through the archeological spadework of psychoanalytic hermeneutics. The first foundation consists in a psychohistorical "construction,"[19] the myth of the primal horde already elaborated in *Totem and Taboo* (1912). The second is a feat of historical reconstruction, pursued with an almost forensic attention to detail, which culminates in two breathtakingly audacious claims: that Moses was an Egyptian, not a Hebrew, and that he did not pass away in Moab, as the Bible reports, but was murdered by his own people. Both foundations are unsound. Freud himself complained, in both the book and his private correspondence, that he had erected a colossus with clay feet.[20] But this colossus—his analysis of monotheistic patriarchal religion and its psychohistorical consequences—has proved to be an enduringly fascinating provocation.

Freud's theses that Moses was an Egyptian and that he was murdered by the Jews flatly contradict the biblical account. They thus posit a diametrical opposition between historical and symbolic truth, between the historical and the symbolic Moses. This is all the more paradoxical when one considers that not a single scrap of evidence for the historical Moses has come down to us. Apart from the Moses of the Bible, all we have to go on is a couple of Hellenistic and Jewish legends of even more dubious historicity, and these barely figure in Freud's account. The contradiction he constructs is not one between biblical and extrabiblical sources, but one that lies within the Bible itself. The biblical Moses is a man with two faces, a palimpsest, a carefully retouched portrait. In Freud's view, the biblical report takes great pains to cover up the two basic facts of Moses' Egyptian ethnicity and his murder, even as it betrays itself in the traces that, despite everything, are left standing. One such trace is the name Moses, an obviously Egyptian name, which the biblical report fits out with a threadbare Hebrew etymology. Another is the legendary tale of his infancy, which places the familiar mythological scheme of the "hero's birth" (Otto Rank) on its head in such a way as to force the conclusion that an Egyptian is here being "Judaized." A third trace is Moses' "heavy tongue," which indicates that he was unable to speak fluent Hebrew and had to rely on a translator, Aaron, to communicate with the Jews.[21] The alleged murder of Moses likewise left behind several traces in the Bible. Freud sees such traces in the murderous violence and openly homicidal threats frequently directed at Moses, as well as in the topos of the violent destiny of the prophets, particularly in Hosea, from which first Goethe and then the Old Testament scholar Ernst Sellin, whom Freud cites as an authority, deduced that Moses must have been murdered. In Exodus 17:4, for example, it is written: "And Moses cried unto the Lord, saying, What shall I do unto this people? they be almost ready to stone me." And in Numbers 14:10, we read: "But all the congregation bade stone them [Moses and Aaron] with stones." Many other prophets in Israel, all the way down to John the Baptist and Jesus, suffered the same fate. The "violent destiny of the prophets" is a recurring motif in biblical writings.[22] The key text here is Isaiah 53, which depicts the tribulations endured by god's servant. From these traces, Freud concluded that Moses was slain by the Jews because they found it impossible, in the long term, to meet the stringent requirements imposed upon them by his abstract, spiritualized religion. Progress in intellectuality, and the sense of superiority it brings with it, always precipitates reactionary violence. Moses was its first victim, and in this sense one could say that the Jews who killed him were the first anti-Semites.[23] For anti-Semitism—a particularly pressing concern for Freud at the time he wrote the book—is a reaction against intellect, which this world is prepared to tolerate only grudgingly. Anti-Semitism is anti-monotheism, hence anti-intellectualism. Moses' personal responsibility for creating the Jewish people becomes all the more evident once it is demonstrated that he was an Egyptian by birth, and that the monotheistic religion he preached therefore had nothing that the Jews had brought with them from their own tradition to draw upon. Abraham is then simply the figure of a retroactive fiction of continuity. The Jews owe their existence as a people to an impulse from outside.

For Freud, Moses was a supporter of Akhenaten who passed on monotheistic religion to the Jews living in the Delta and emigrated with them to Palestine after the Pharaoh's death. Yet the Jews proved unequal to the high intellectual and spiritual demands placed on them by abstract monotheism, killing Moses and then covering up what they had done. Their collective deed was a traumatic experience because they acted out in it the repressed memory of the murder of the primal father, a memory that goes all the way back to the beginnings of phylogenesis.[24] The murder of Moses signified "the awakening of the forgotten memory-trace by a recent real repetition of the event. The murder of Moses was a repetition of this kind."[25] Moses' monotheism thus amounted to the return of the father, and the murder of Moses repeated the primal father's own demise at the hands of his sons. The paradox at the heart of Freud's argument is that Moses could only become what he is—"the creator of the Jewish people," a figure of lasting and indelible memory—by being murdered and the memory of the crime then being repressed. After his murder, the monotheism he preached entered a period of latency lasting several centuries before finally returning to cast its spell over the masses. The idea of a possible connection between these two events—the repressed murder on the one hand, the return of the repressed on the other—raises the problem of the difference in time that separates them. Whereas Akhenaten lived in the fourteenth century BCE, the development of biblical monotheism did not really get under way until the prophetic movement of the eighth century, first breaking through to the pure and radical monotheism understood by Freud under the term "monotheistic religion" in post-exilic times. The Freudian interpretation sets out to explain this delay by positing a phase of latency. The theory of repression contends that there is such a thing as a preserving forgetfulness. According to Freud, the idea of exclusive monotheism was cloaked by this preserving forgetfulness, which allowed it to be retained by the Jews from the fourteenth all the way through to the fifth century BCE.

For Freud, the murder of Moses was thus important precisely because it was repressed; it could only help bring about the eventual breakthrough of monotheism among the Jews thanks to the irresistible dynamic proper to the return of the repressed. Just as the murder of the primal father put an end to the system of the primal horde and became the founding act (or founding crime) of culture and totemic religion, so the murder of Moses put an end to polytheistic religion and became the founding act (or founding crime) of monotheism. Every truly compelling, spiritually captivating tradition rests on an act of repression and has, to put it crudely, a skeleton in the closet. Only psychoanalysis can reach down to this depth dimension of collective spiritual life to uncover an origin that has not just slipped from conscious memory (i.e., written transmission), but has, according to all the rules of psychoanalytic theory, been repressed as a deeply traumatic experience.

The question now arises as to where exactly this split into surface and depth is assumed to have occurred. Is it to be located in the psychic structure of the individual, in this case the Jewish soul, which remains unconsciously aware of its complicity in a homicide it has repressed at the conscious level? Or is it instead to be found in the cultural memory of written and oral tradition, which contains, beneath its surface meaning, a deeper meaning accessible only in traces? Jacques Derrida and Richard Bernstein both defend Freud against Yerushalmi's charge of psycho-Lamarckism by referring Freud's theory of unconscious transference to cultural institutions like the "archive" (Derrida) and "tradition" (Bernstein). But Freud unambiguously and explicitly makes his position clear on this point, siding *against* the cultural archive and *in favor of* psycho-Lamarckism in the summary that concludes the first part of his study on Moses. The passage deserves to be quoted at some length:

When we study the reactions to early traumas, we are quite often surprised to find that they are not strictly limited to what the subject himself has really experienced but diverge from it in a way that fits in much better with the model of a phylogenetic event and, in general, can only be explained by such an influence. The behavior of neurotic children towards their parents in the Oedipus and castration complex abounds in such reactions, which seem unjustified in the individual case and only become intelligible phylogenetically—by their connection with the experience of earlier generations. It would be well worth while to place this material, which I am able to appeal to here, before the public in a collected form. Its evidential value seems to me strong enough for me to venture on a further step and to posit the assertion that the archaic heritage of human beings comprises not only dispositions but also subject-matter—memory-traces of the experience of earlier generations. In this way the compass as well as the importance of the archaic heritage would be significantly extended.

On further reflection I must admit that I have behaved for a long time as though the inheritance of memory-traces of the experience of our ancestors, independently of direct communication and of the influence of education by the setting of an example, were established beyond question. When I spoke of the survival of a tradition among a people or of the formation of a people's character, I had mostly in mind an inherited tradition of this kind and not one transmitted by communication. Or at least I made no distinction between the two and was not clearly aware of my audacity in neglecting to do so. My position, no doubt, is made more difficult by the present attitude of biological science, which refuses to hear of the inheritance of acquired characters by succeeding generations. I must, however, in all modesty confess that nevertheless I cannot do without this factor in biological evolution. The same thing is not in question, indeed, in the two cases: in the one it is a matter of acquired characters which are hard to grasp, in the other of memory-traces of external events—something tangible, as it were. But it may well be that at bottom we cannot imagine one without the other.

If we assume the survival of these memory-traces in the archaic heritage, we have bridged the gulf between individual and group psychology: we can deal with peoples as we do with an individual neurotic.[26]

That is a clear vote for biology and against culture. Mnemohistory, by contrast, confines itself to the archive of cultural transmission. It can do without phylogenetic primal memories. My criticism of Freud is that he had too weak a concept of cultural memory (or the cultural archive) when he confined it to the *mémoire volontaire* of consciously transmitted messages:

A tradition that was based only on communication could not lead to the compulsive character that attaches to religious phenomena. It would be listened to, judged, and perhaps dismissed, like any other piece of information from outside; it would never attain the privilege of being liberated from the constraint of logical thought. It must have undergone the fate of being repressed, the condition of lingering in the unconscious, before it is able to display such powerful effects on its return, to bring the masses under its spell, as we have seen with astonishment and hitherto without comprehension in the case of religious tradition.[27]

The archives of cultural transmission are multi-layered and preserve much that is no longer understood in its original meaning and function. There is no better example of this than Moses himself, with his Egyptian name and its Hebrew etymology ("he who was drawn from the water"). Another example would be the deferred memory of both the Amarna and the Hyksos periods in the legend of the lepers. Cultural memory is not just a *mémoire volontaire*, but a *mémoire involontaire* as well; much is contained in its lower strata that can break out again and seize hold of people's imagination after a long phase of latency.

The trauma of monotheism, if there is such a thing, rests in my opinion not on a twofold parricide, whose victims were first the primal father and then Moses, but on a twofold deicide, whose victims were first the "pagan" gods and then the god of monotheism himself. The theoclastic violence that inheres within monotheism, that is to say, is ultimately directed against god himself. Not just negative theology, but even the death of god lie down the path of a progress in intellectuality.

The Ban on Graven Images as
Progress in Intellectuality

Freud saw the decisive breakthrough or advance in intellectuality in the ban on graven images:

Among the precepts of the Moses religion there is one that is of greater importance than appears to begin with. This is the prohibition against making an image of god—the compulsion to worship a god whom one cannot see. In this, I suspect, Moses was outdoing the strictness of the Aten religion. Perhaps he merely wanted to be consistent: his god would in that case have neither a name nor a countenance. Perhaps it was a fresh measure against magical abuses. But if this prohibition were accepted, it must have a profound effect. For it meant that a sensory perception was given second place to what may be called an abstract idea—a triumph of intellectuality over sensuality or, strictly speaking, an instinctual renunciation, with all its necessary psychological consequences.[28]

For Freud, this Mosaic ban signified the breakthrough to a new world. "The new realm of intellectuality was opened up."[29] The rejection of images, and nothing else, unlocked the gates to a new kingdom of the spirit. Freud understood the second commandment as proclaiming god's absolute invisibility and unrepresentability. Given that the commandment forbids images as such and not just those of god, one would today be inclined to foreground Yahweh's singularity and the demand that he be worshipped exclusively. Each and every image, so the idea goes, bears within it the potential to be worshipped as a god. This would necessarily be an "other god," since the true god cannot be depicted.[30] Freud's interpretation of the ban on graven images stands in a long tradition, however. The ban was understood in this way even in classical antiquity. According to Hecataeus of Abdera, who lived in the second half of the fourth century BCE, Moses banned divine images because he was "of the opinion that God is not in human form; rather the Heaven that surrounds the earth is alone divine, and rules the universe."[31] The true religion instituted by Moses consists in the monotheistic and imageless worship of a single, "all-encompassing" (*peri-echon*) god of the heavens. In Strabo's account (first century BCE), an Egyptian priest called Moses decided to leave his country and emigrate to Judea with many who shared his dissatisfaction with the Egyptian religion. He taught that god is "the thing which we call heaven, or universe, or the nature of all that exists."[32] This divine being cannot be reproduced in any image: "Nay, people should leave off all image-carving, and . . . should worship God without an image." All that is required to walk close to god is to "live self-restrained and righteous lives." For Strabo, progress in intellectuality thus means first and foremost an ethicization of religion. The god of Moses eschews bloody sacrifices and orgiastic dances; what he demands in their stead is righteousness. To be sure, Strabo has only the decalogue in mind here. In his opinion, the Hebrews subsequently fell away from the pure teaching of Moses, developing superstitious customs such as dietary laws, circumcision, and other observances.[33] As we shall see, the link between imagelessness and ethics is important for Freud as well. One of Freud's forerunners in the project of a genealogy of Judaism, John Toland, bases his reconstruction of Jewish origins in his text of the same name (*Origines Judaicae*, 1709) on Strabo's report.[34] Tacitus (first century CE) likewise characterizes the Jewish idea of god as monotheistic and aniconic: "The Egyptians worship many animals and monstrous images; the Jews conceive of one god only, and that with the mind only [*mente sola*]: they regard as impious those who make from perishable materials representations of gods in man's image; that supreme and eternal being is to them incapable of representation and without end."[35]

For Freud, belief in divine election lies at the heart of Jewish identity. This belief, and the pride associated with it, are sustained by the ban on graven images and the renunciation of instinctual impulses it requires. The ban on images implies the three fundamental principles of monotheistic religion, as these are defined by Freud: "the idea of a single god, as well as the rejection of magically effective ceremonial and the stress upon ethical demands made in his name."[36] The connection of the ban on graven images with ethics, or rather the connection of idolatry with lawlessness, fornication, and violence, is deeply etched into the biblical tradition. The prophets reject (or at least relativize) the cult of sacrificial offerings and call in the first place for righteousness. The law—and here this means the stipulations of ethics—is declared to be the will of god and presented as the sole means for leading a life that is pleasing unto him. Freud's concept of progress in intellectuality links the ban on graven images to the renunciation of instinct. The ban on images involves turning away from the senses and towards the spirit. Monotheism, in Freud's eyes, is a feat of sublimation. It implies the same "no to the world" that I also see at work in the ban on graven images and in monotheism as such, and about which my critics among Old Testament scholars profess to know nothing. I reiterate my standpoint once again because I do not intend it as a critique of monotheism but, on the contrary, as a thoroughly appreciative recognition of a breakthrough (albeit one that is continually under threat and has often been revoked) or "progress" in intellectuality. Whoever obeys the laws lives as a stranger here on earth. Thus we read in Ps. 119:19: "I am a stranger in the earth: hide not thy commandments from me." Staying true to the law means living as a stranger on earth, even in the Promised Land. The law circumscribes a counterfactual order that compels its people to dwell in the world without entirely being assimilated to it. Monotheism fosters an existential unhomeliness. This estrangement from the world is what is meant by "progress in intellectuality."

It will readily be conceded that Freud's interpretation of the ban on graven images as a breakthrough in progress in intellectuality and as a centerpiece of Jewish identity and pride has considerable inner plausibility. On the other hand, one could object that this Jewish step from the realm of the senses to the realm of the spirit, far from representing a unique case, must be seen as belonging (albeit in a unique way) in the context of the general breakthrough in human history that Karl Jaspers called the "axial age."[37]

The first name that should be mentioned here is, of course, Plato's. The Platonic philosophy is the most concerted attempt to escape from the world of sensory appearance into the world of a truth that only the eyes of the spirit are fit to apprehend. In this respect, it paved the way for countless philosophical and religious movements based on the idea of a higher spiritual world, notably Neoplatonism, Hermeticism, and, above all, Gnosticism. Western thought has been profoundly shaped by the Platonic philosophy of spirit, and even Freud's own text is indebted to Platonic motifs. Yet, curiously, Freud makes no mention of Plato. Like Heine, he constructs his concept of a progress in intellectuality by opposing the Jews to the Greeks: "The pre-eminence given to intellectual labours throughout some two thousand years in the life of the Jewish people has, of course, had its effect. It has helped to check the brutality and the tendency to violence which are apt to appear where the development of muscular strength is the popular ideal." Freud is well aware that "the development of muscular strength" does not quite do justice to the Greek "popular ideal"; he therefore continues: "Harmony in the cultivation of intellectual and physical activity, such as was achieved by the Greek people, was denied to the Jews." And he concludes by asserting: "In this dichotomy their decision was at least in favour of the worthier alternative."[38]

If one asks in what area the Greeks have most lastingly influenced the West and where, within the Greek tradition, the West could identify an origin, one would have to point to Platonic and Aristotelian metaphysics. Sport and fitness cultures are relatively recent innovations, which, while they may well number among the essential elements of our contemporary Western identity, have no place in the old European tradition. On the other hand, it has become clear since Nietzsche, at the latest, that Plato's two-worlds doctrine may have imported into Greek thought a dualism that was originally foreign to it. Plato had an enormous influence, to be sure, but he cannot be regarded as a representative exponent of Greek culture. Put drastically, he belonged on the side of Heine's Jews. Not without reason did the Pythagorean Numenius of Apamaeia call Plato "an Attic-speaking Moses." So perhaps Freud was right to ignore him, and to grant the Jews a special place in the history of humankind's progress in intellectuality.[39]

More striking in this respect, however, is his estimation of Christianity. For him, this religion signifies a clear decline in intellectuality, because it returned to images and magic rites, especially the sacrificial rite of the totem meal in which god himself is incorporated into the community of believers.[40] This simplistic outsider's perspective can be explained in part by Freud's experience of Christianity, presumably largely confined to the popular Catholicism practiced in Vienna, in part by his reading of authors such as W. Stevenson Smith, Charles Darwin, and James Frazer.

The fact that the external forms of Austrian popular Catholicism aroused displeasure, if not downright disgust, in a Jewish observer is quite understandable, just as Western anti-Judaism took issue precisely with the outward forms of Judaism. It is only natural that interreligious aversions are fueled by the rites of others rather than being informed by theological insider perspectives, to which the observer ordinarily lacks access. Indeed, from an insider perspective, it must be said that Christianity is primarily and fundamentally distinguished by a principle that could no more aptly be characterized than with Freud's phrase, "progress in intellectuality." One is tempted to say that, in coining this phrase, Freud resorted to a Christian cliché rather than a Platonic one. Yet I suspect that his use of a Christian topos was quite intentional, and not without a certain irony. For the idea of an advance in spirituality numbers among the standard elements of Christian anti-Judaism, drawn on time and again to justify Christianity's rejection of the law. The Pauline critique of the law argues with the concepts of spirit and flesh. The letter kills, but the spirit gives life. This motif runs through the entire Christian tradition. The Halacha is dismissed as "justice through works," and hence as external and material. The law stands opposed to belief, directed towards a kingdom of god that can be attained by neither the senses nor reason alone. *Credo quia absurdum*—Freud cites this archetypal Christian formula on two occasions in this context without seeing any contradiction between it and his appraisal of Christianity. According to the Christian view of things, the Jews remain mired in the flesh: *Israel carnalis.*[41] Only by exiting the world of the law can one gain entry to the kingdom of the spirit.

This incessant insistence on spirituality in Christian theology, going all the way back to the teachings of Jesus and Saint Paul, could no more have escaped Freud's notice than his own indebtedness to this intellectual tradition. It therefore seems much more plausible to me that he wanted to snatch this central Christian theologumen from the Christians and credit the Jews with it, in ironic inversion of the Christian propensity for declaring central Jewish motifs such as neighborly love, love of the enemy, the emphasis on the inner self, and so on, to be specifically Christian achievements. That is why he applies the Pauline formula, intended to legitimize the Christian rejection of the law, to the ban on graven images and the Jewish rejection of divine images. Christianity "took up components from many other sources, renounced a number of characteristics of pure monotheism and adapted itself in many details to the rituals of the other Mediterranean peoples." It thereby returned in a certain sense to Egypt: "It was as though Egypt was taking vengeance once more on the heirs of Akhenaten."[42] Freud expresses himself even more clearly in another passage:

In some respects the new religion meant a cultural regression as compared with the older, Jewish one, as regularly happens when a new mass of people, of a lower level, break their way in or are given admission. The Christian religion did not maintain the high level in things of the mind to which Judaism had soared. It was no longer strictly monotheist, it took over numerous symbolic rituals from surrounding peoples, it re-established the great mother-goddess and found room to introduce many of the divine figures of polytheism only lightly veiled, though in subordinate positions. Above all, it did not, like the Aten religion and the Mosaic one which followed it, exclude the entry of superstitions, magical and mystical elements, which were to prove a severe inhibition upon the intellectual development of the next two thousand years.[43]

Freud refuses to acknowledge the Christian radicalization of religious spirituality as evidence of progress in intellectuality. "It happens later on," he writes in relation to the rise of Christianity, "that intellectuality itself is overpowered by the very puzzling emotional phenomenon of faith. Here we have the celebrated *Credo quia absurdum.*"[44] Rather than identifying a further advance in intellectuality in this development, Freud thus equates it, on the contrary, with an exit from intellectuality. With the rejection of reason as unspiritual or insufficiently spiritual, the border to mysticism, which Freud conflates with magic, and which, for him, has nothing whatsoever to do with intellectuality, has been crossed. In his eyes, (Jewish) intellectuality and (Christian) spirituality are two entirely different things. What he means by "progress in intellectuality" bears a close resemblance to Max Weber's theorem of a "disenchantment of the world" through rationalization.[45] In this respect, Christianity signifies a step in the opposite direction of a reenchantment of the world. For the same reason, Freud is equally incapable of recognizing Platonic, Gnostic, or Hermetic mysticism as an advance in intellectuality. Yet according to their own self-understanding, these movements were pursuing exactly this goal. The whole domain of cultic ritual was to be internalized and transformed into a spiritual activity called *thysia logikē*, "intellectual sacrifice."[46] Logos means reason, and the phrase *thysia logikē* could equally be rendered "religion of reason." Philosophical mysticism thought of itself as a highly rational business. In late antiquity, the entire Mediterranean world found itself gripped by this longing for intellectualization, and many of the movements that emerged at the time were to exert an incalculable influence on the intellectual history of the West for centuries to come. The distinction between intellectuality and spirituality simply cannot be upheld from the insider perspective of Christian religion, nor indeed from that of its numerous philosophical and mystical offshoots and rivals (including the Jewish Kabbala).

All this could be held against Freud's construction of a Jewish head start in progress in intellectuality, and thus a Jewish origin of the West. Yet for all that, there is equally a sense in which he was right to derive "the religion of reason from the sources of Judaism," to quote the title of another book that likewise postulates a Jewish origin of the West.[47] Even though it may not initially have been intended this way, the ban on graven images contains an eminently rational impulse that first came to the fore in later interpretations, particularly in the form of religious satire. This form of the critique of religion has its roots in the Jewish ban on graven images, and it is unmistakably continued by Freud in his book on Moses, principally in its pathological imagery. With the ban on images, the distinction between true and false in the divine world, and with it the distinction between reason and madness, enters religion for the first time.[48] The "Mosaic prohibition" constructs an Archimedian point from which iconic religion can be unmasked as an illusion, and from which Freud can ultimately unmask religion itself as illusory. Progress in intellectuality consists in our gradual emancipation from the constraints of idolatry, which hold our minds in captivity. In revisiting the ban on graven images, Freud reveals this striving for intellectual emancipation to be a deeply Jewish project and, at the same time, a tradition that he himself claims to inherit and take a step further with his psychoanalysis. If it is the mission of humankind to advance in intellectuality, then the Jews are to be found marching at the forefront.

CHAPTER 5

The Psychohistorical Consequences
of Monotheism

I want to conclude by summarizing in four points some of the psychohistorical consequences of monotheism (or counterreligion), as they appear to me from the perspective of a theory of cultural memory and mnemohistory.

The "Scriptural Turn": From Cult to Book

The shift from primary to secondary religious experience can be understood as a shift from ritual to text. Whereas, in primary or archaic religions, the text is embedded in ritual and subordinated to it, in monotheism the text (in the form of canonized writings) assumes cardinal importance, and ritual is reduced to a supporting and supplementary role. The turn from one to the other acts as a watershed, separating two types of religion, which could be contrasted as cult religions and book religions. The latter include the three Western monotheisms of Judaism, Christianity, and Islam, as well as Buddhism, Jainism, and the Sikh religion. All secondary religions are religions of the book. They are based on a canon of sacred texts like the Hebrew Bible, the Christian Bible, the Koran, the Jaina canon, the Pali canon, and the Adi Granth.[1] The monotheistic turn has its correlate in a change of medium. Writing and transcendence belong together on the side of secondary religions, just as ritual and immanence belong together on the side of primary religions. Over two hundred years ago, Moses Mendelssohn was already drawing attention to this connection between religious history and the history of writing: "It seems to me that the change that has occurred in different periods of culture with regard to written characters has had, at all times, a very important part in the revolutions of human knowledge in general, and in the various modifications of men's opinions and ideas about religious matters, in particular."[2] What Mendelssohn had in mind at the time (following in the footsteps of William Warburton and Giambattista Vico) was the transition from pictographic to alphabetic writing,[3] whereas I am principally concerned here with the transition from orality to scripturality, from "ritual" to "textual continuity."[4]

Interlinked with the principle of ritual continuity is the idea that the world needs to be held on its course. Ritual cultures or cult religions typically operate on the assumption that the universe would suffer, or even come to an end, if the rites ceased to be observed in the prescribed fashion. Rituals always serve to prop up a cosmic order otherwise threatened with collapse. Textual continuity emerges when this idea starts to lose its force. For the Bible, this change is brought about by the rise of a theology of creation and a theology of the will. The world owes its continued existence, not to the performance of any rites, but to the preserving will and workings of a transcendent god. The principle of ritual continuity and the requirement that the world be held on its course have their correlate in the social type of the priest, just as the social type of the exegete, scholar and preacher pertains to the principle of textual interpretation. Strict purity laws separate the priest from the group. The ritual purity by which he distinguishes himself from the rest of the community must be won through washing, fasting, sexual abstinence, and other forms of "magical ascesis" (Max Weber). In the first place, then, his fitness for the priesthood is a physical matter; the body is implicated here to a much greater extent than in the case of book religions.

The transition from cult religions to book religions is accompanied by a structural transformation of the sacred.[5] Primary or cult religions have to do with the sacred as it is made manifest in the world (*hieros, sacer*). The sacred with which the priest comes into contact after ritually cleansing himself exists within the world. Embodied or brought to visible presence in a particular place, it is separated by very high barriers from the profane world of the everyday. Contact with the sacred on the part of the priest demands holiness in the sense of *hosios, sanctus*. This denotes a state cut off from the sphere of the profane. Secondary religions, by contrast, cancel out this distinction, since for them, the sacred is no longer to be found in the world. The only thing that still counts as *hieros* or *sacer* is holy scripture, *biblia sacra*. That is why, in Judaism and Islam, the book is invested with ideas and laws that are clearly of ritual origin. Thus Jews, for example, are forbidden to put a Bible on the ground, and Muslims are permitted neither to destroy something written in the Arabic script and language nor to take it with them to be read in unseemly places, even if the text in question is only a newspaper. Christianity, and Protestantism in particular, cast aside these last remainders of ritual. The exegete or preacher qualifies for his position through his intimate knowledge of the sacred texts. He knows how to read and recite them, he knows them by heart and can illuminate one passage with reference to others, and above all, he knows how to make them relevant to the lived reality of the present. Here, direct interaction with nature is out of the question. The success with which he carries out his office can be gauged by the degree to which his sermon is taken to heart by the congregation, that is, the degree to which the lessons of holy scripture are translated into everyday conduct and implemented in everyday life.

The psychohistorical consequences of this flight of the sacred from the world—on the one hand into transcendence, on the other into scripture—result in a fundamental shift of attention. Once directed at appearances in the world and the sacred that manifests itself in those appearances, attention is now transferred entirely to scripture. Everything else is deemed idolatrous. The things of this world, especially images, represent traps designed to lure the mind away from scripture. It is the duty of the faithful to guard against stumbling into these traps. The demonization of images and the visual domain is accompanied by a linguistic reform that seeks to desensualize religion and dismantle the theatricality of ritual. Moses Mendelssohn had a clear view of these consequences as well. "We are *literati, men of letters*," he laments. "Our whole being depends on letters."[6] He praises the Jewish law precisely because, by prescribing so many rituals, it salvages the aesthetic dimension of religion under the conditions of book religion.

The principle of ritual continuity is based on media that bring the sacred to visual presence in the world. These include holy places, trees, springs, rocks, grottos, and groves, but also, and in the first place, pictures, statues, symbols and architectural installations such as temples, pyramids, and stupas. The priest must modify his behavior upon entering the sphere of sacred presence. "Put off thy shoes from thy feet," we read in Exodus 3:5, "for the place upon which thou standest is holy ground." Where the sacred is physically and visibly present, other laws hold sway that can have fatal consequences for those who choose to flout them. This holds true for sacred texts as well, which are embedded into rituals so that they may be recited during the service. They, too, bring the sacred to presence. Correctly recited in the right place, at the right time, and by the right speaker, they unleash cosmogonic forces that help keep the world on its course. In late period Egypt, these texts were summarized under the generic title "power of Re," which means something like "solar energy." Egyptian priests had to chew on soda and cleanse their mouths before reciting these texts, which were to be kept in strict secrecy and protected from profanation in the same way as the holy places, images, and symbols.

In Judaism, the relationship between writing and cult is reversed. Here, writing no longer serves to choreograph or record cultic practice. Writing is what matters more than anything else. Cultic enactment is reduced to the reenactment of scripture, in the form of common reading, remembrance, avowal, and exegesis. That amounts to a complete volteface. Rather than being used to stabilize ritual, writing takes its place.

The Jewish historian Josephus Flavius had already grasped the key difference between "ritual" and "textual" continuity when he contrasted Judaism with Hellenism (that is, paganism):

Could there be a more saintly government than that? Could God be more worthily honoured than by such a scheme, under which religion is the end and aim of the training of the entire community, the priests are entrusted with the special charge of it, and the whole administration of the state resembles some sacred ceremony? Practices which, under the name of mysteries and rites of initiation, other nations are unable to observe for but a few days, we maintain with delight and unflinching determination all our lives.[7]

While the pagans are obliged to wait until the next performance of their rites, the Jews enjoy permanent possession of their cultural texts, having been initiated into them and instructed about them by their priests. Their "mysteries"—the reading of these texts guided by sacerdotal exegesis—are permanent and ongoing.

It is one of the most remarkable coincidences in history that the Jewish temple was destroyed at precisely the moment when the inner development of the Jewish religion had rendered it superfluous. Scripture had already been installed in its place, and the meaning of the rites hollowed out from within, when Titus laid waste to the temple in the year 70 CE. The Jesus movement was only one of many Jewish (and also Greek) movements that sought to abolish the basic idea of cult religion—namely, blood sacrifice or ritual slaughter—through sublimation, ethicization, and interiorization. Had Titus spared the temple, it would have had to be shut down—either that, or Judaism, and thus Christianity and Islam as well, would never have arisen. The temple had outlived its usefulness, for the cult that it housed had long since been laid to rest in the graveyard of scripture.

There is much to suggest that Jewish monotheism, the principle of revelation, and the growing abhorrence of traditional forms of cultic practice that flowed from this principle, were all born from the spirit of scripture, or at least are fundamentally linked to the medium of writing. Moses Mendelssohn saw this connection between media revolutions and religious transformations more than two hundred years ago. The step into the religion of transcendence was a step out of the world—one could almost speak in this context of an "exodus"—into scripture.[8] Canonized scripture ultimately replaces art, public life, and the world. The world as such is declared to be an object of idolatry and discredited. Worship of the creator cannot become entangled in his creation. The radical otherworldliness of god corresponds to the radical scripturality of his revelation.

With that, we have touched on a connection between writing and transcendence that Friedrich Kittler has summarized with inimitable succinctness: "Without cultural technologies . . . , we would never know that there is anything other than what there is. The sky would simply be the sky, earth would be earth, and so-called humans would simply be men and women. But revelations of the sacred result in knowledge, or more precisely, *artificial intelligence.*"[9] The Bible and the Koran did not originate in cultic formulae, but in laws and stories. At bottom, their normativity is moral and legal rather than theurgic in nature. They provide a foundation for a way of life, not for cultic practice. Scripture stands opposed to cult and spells its end. What the eighteenth century called "positive religion," contrasting it with "natural religion" as something artificial, would have been unthinkable without the cultural technologies of writing and hermeneutics. Prophetic monotheism lacks natural evidence; it walks, as Saint Paul says, not in vision but in faith. Faith is supported by scripture, by the covenant, and by law. Cult draws on ritual enactment, performance, and vision. Scripture leads to a deritualization and detheatricalization of religion.

Into the Crypt

Secondary religious experience cannot be reduced to an unambiguously negative relationship to the "false consciousness" of paganism. It is far more complicated than that, taking up forms and elements of primary religious experience in a process of syncretistic amalgamation. None of the new or secondary religions succeeded in completely wiping out the vestiges of the primary religion or religions on which they were built; rather, they frequently adopted such traces and adapted them to their own purposes. Indeed, Theo Sundermeier argues that the extent to which they did so determined their assimilatory force and their capacity to win converts: "The history of religion does not proceed in such a way that primary religious experience is superseded by the new experience pioneered by the visionaries and founders of secondary religions. It is rather the case that in a third phase, a complex process of repudiation and symbolic reintegration, the vital elements of primary religious experience are integrated and fused into a new synthesis. Here we find an organic syncretism at work that is both inevitable and unobjectionable. The more this synthesis succeeds, the greater are the chances that the new religion will be able to establish itself as a viable popular religion."[10]

The "pagan" origin of these "vital elements," however, has to be forgotten and made invisible. One could therefore say that secondary or counterreligions develop a new form of unconsciousness by enriching themselves with elements of primary religious experience and religious practice, while at the same time having to reinterpret their semantics and refunction their forms to fit them to the new context. These elements constitute a kind of "crypt" in the edifice of secondary religions, a subterranean realm no longer illuminated by the light of consciously cultivated religious semantics, from whose depths, however, new (or rather age-old) impulses can arise at any time to bring people under their spell.

This recalls Sigmund Freud's theory of religion. As we have seen, Freud describes the rise of monotheistic religion as a case of the "return of the repressed." For him, too, the history of religion presents itself as a stratification of memory. The lowest stratum or deepest "crypt" is represented by what he calls the "archaic legacy," the patri-oedipal imprint left behind by the "primal horde." At a later stage of cultural development, the killing was brought to an end and the father elevated to the rank of a divine being. Sacrificial offerings and totemic meals took the place of primal violence. (Primary) religion appeared and buried the terrors of prehistory, which had become sedimented in the unconscious foundation of the human psyche as an "archaic legacy," with its rites and taboos. In the monotheistic message of Moses the Egyptian, patriarchal religion, with its strict demands of sublimation and its norms of purity and righteousness, reemerged from the unconscious in a new guise. The "murder of Moses" was a case of acted out, unrecollected history, which inscribed itself as a traumatic experience in the Jewish soul and, after a period of latency lasting centuries, broke through in the monotheistic message of the prophet with all the force of a "return of the repressed."

To be sure, Freud's distinction between "totemism" and "monotheism" sounds quite different to the distinction between primary and secondary religions, and few today would subscribe without reservation to his mythology of the "primal horde" and the murder of Moses. One could consign this theory without further ado to the museum of scientific mythmaking, were it not for the deeply persuasive insights into the depth dimensions of cultural memory that it generates. This form of memory cannot be reduced to the conscious business of tradition and reception,[11] but operates in fits and starts, spurts and breaks, latencies and returns. Above all, it is never entirely realized in the present, but brings forth ever-new syntheses of old and new. The forms of primary religious experience that have fused with secondary religions could be characterized as an "archaic legacy" in a quite different sense than Freud's. While it may not have been inscribed into the human psyche, it nonetheless forms a depth dimension, a "crypt" of religious tradition, which, like language, bears within it much more knowledge and many more memories than those who live in that tradition can ever fully bring to consciousness.

The idea that biblical monotheism is a two-sided or duplicitous religion, split between an exterior or upper side formulated in its canonic texts and a concealed interior or underside, has a long history. I have already discussed, in chapter 3, the theory of religion developed by the Jewish philosopher Maimonides, and I want to come back to it in this context. When, in the twelfth century, Maimonides set himself the task of finding an explanation for the Mosaic ritual laws, using the principle of "normative inversion" as a guideline, he contended that monotheistic religion contains a depth dimension into which paganism, repulsed and then forgotten, had been pushed. For Maimonides, it goes without saying that those who practice the law are no longer aware of its original pagan countermeaning. Religious scholarship first shed light on these depths, and Maimonides, with his rediscovery of paganism or Sabianism, has a fair claim to be considered the founding father of this discipline.[12] He explained the function of the ritual laws as an art of forgetting,[13] a withdrawal cure from Sabian idolatry. The law, or rather the entire biblical religion as a complicated praxis of cult custom, rites, and practical rules, assumes a double aspect in the light of this theory. It appears as the historical, time-bound vessel of a timeless truth, which it conceals within itself, and which will only prevail after a long process of purification, once the hold of idolatry has been broken and the community has returned to an unsullied knowledge of god. Maimonides therefore calls the laws *divrej kfilayim* ("words of reduplication," or in Spencer's translation, "verba duplicata").[14] They have an obvious meaning and a hidden meaning. The Sabian rites, by contrast, have no other meaning than the publicly available one that lies on the surface. Through the structure of antagonistic superimposition or superscription onto a rejected tradition, religion takes on a double aspect. The parallel to Sundermeier's distinction between primary and secondary religious experience and the concept of counterreligion is clear. Secondary religions or counterreligions are duplicitous: they bear encrypted within themselves the paganism they ostensibly reject.

The Invention of the Inner Self

It is typical of secondary religions, as Theo Sundermeier in particular has emphasized,[15] that they are aware of their own novelty. Needless to say, the monotheistic religions of Judaism, Christianity, and Islam do not think of themselves as secondary or counterreligions. In their view, the only original religion is monotheism, and the foundational work of Moses, Jesus, and Mohammed signifies nothing less than a return to a monotheistic truth that had since been overgrown with errors. All the more remarkable, then, the emphatic precision with which the Exodus myth depicts the transition from primary to secondary religion. With this transition, described by the Jewish and Christian tradition as an epochal shift from *ante legem* to *sub lege*, religion makes a quantum leap. It places itself on a strict normative footing (the laws); it sharply delimits itself from its own other, a process for which "Egypt" and "Canaan" stand as the central symbols; and it gives itself the form of a "covenant" (*b'rît*), modeled on a political alliance, according to which Israel not only agrees to become the people of god, but god likewise vows to become the god of a people. It makes little sense here to talk of a return to the source. Something radically new is being created. I understand the entire Exodus-and-Sinai complex as the narrative account of this conversion from primary to secondary religion, from a lower to a higher state of consciousness, allegiance, and commitment.

Through their awareness of their own novelty, secondary religions at the same time become aware of themselves as religions in a new, emphatic sense of the term, unknown to primary religions. Primary religions do not separate themselves from something else, and they therefore have no need to distinguish themselves from "culture" or to "sectorally segregate" themselves within culture. Secondary or counterreligions foster a higher degree of consciousness because the distinction between true and false on which they rest must continually be drawn anew within the soul of the believer. Secondary religions are aware of themselves as religions, not just in opposition to magic, superstition, idolatry, and other forms of "false" religion, but also in contrast to science, art, politics, and other social subsystems. The transition from primary to secondary religious experience is therefore also a consciousness-raising exercise. Whatever was unaware of itself, within the horizon of primary religious experience, as a sphere of autonomous values and norms, now emerges in its specific contours and compels a conscious decision. "Now one can and must decide for the new. It is not enough to go through the motions, inner acceptance is required as well. Belief and discipleship are the order of the day, truth must be separated from lies. . . . Now there is 'true' and 'false' religion."[16]

That is why the transition from primary to secondary religious experience represents a breakthrough in the history of the mind and soul. Sundermeier alludes to this when he speaks of "inner acceptance."[17] The distinction between truth and lies does not just carve up external space, it cuts through the human heart as well, which for the first time becomes the stage upon which the religious dynamic is played out. It may suffice to recall the Shema prayer, which brings god's oneness into the closest possible connection with the intensity of inner acceptance:

Hear, O Israel, the Lord our God is one Lord:
And thou shalt love the Lord thy God with all thine heart, and with all thy soul,
   and with all thy might.
And these words, which I command thee this day, shall be in thine
   heart.   (Deut. 6:4–6)[18]

Counterreligion and the Concept of Sin

In the introduction to his anthology *Die Sagen der Juden* (The Legends of the Jews), Emanuel bin Gorion (Berdyczewski) notes that the essential feature of the legends is "the sense of an ineradicable guilt incurred by all creatures, and the eternal striving to expiate that guilt nonetheless."[19] This feeling of guilt is not what I have in mind when I speculate on whether "sin"—or perhaps one should say: a new concept of sin—entered into the world with the Mosaic distinction. The sense of guilt discussed by bin Gorion is a very widespread phenomenon. Many religions, perhaps all religions, share the idea of a primordial guilt resulting in the loss of an initial paradisiacal situation and the birth of the world as we know it, with all its suffering and death, hardship and labor. The Bible offers two such myths of primordial guilt: Adam and Eve's expulsion from paradise and the great flood. The legend of the flood can also be found in the Mesopotamian, Greek, and many other traditions, while ancient Egyptian and other African myths tell of an original sin committed by humans leading to the separation of heaven and earth, gods and mortals. In this respect, biblical monotheism is no different from pagan religions. There are numerous parallels to the fall and the flood; this concept of sin is thus nothing new and by no means first came into the world with monotheism. The new concept of sin introduced by monotheism is connected with the unprecedented oath of loyalty that binds the One God who stands over and against the world to his people, or at any rate those of them who believe in him. To sin is to betray that pledge and commit a breach of faith.

The primal scene of this new form of sinfulness is not to be found in the fall and flood, but in the dance around the Golden Calf. With this act, the Israelites betrayed their god and lapsed back into primary religion. Following the exodus from Egypt, primary religion (now stamped as 'paganism') is no longer simply regarded as erroneous, but viewed as a matter of apostasy and sin as well. The boundary between truth and lies has moral as well as cognitive significance. While the false gods may not exist, they nonetheless represent an ever-present source of temptation, lying in wait to beguile the human heart with their snares. Sin arises in conjunction with secondary religious experience as the awareness of having lacked fidelity, the strength of inner resolve, and succumbed to the temptations of false gods. Knowing no distinction between religion and culture, primary religious experience is marked by a plain, almost matter-of-fact evidence. No one would ever contemplate denying the existence of divine forces. They are there for all to see, in the form of sun and moon, air and water, earth and fire, death and life, war and peace. They can be neglected, insufficiently venerated, sinned against in a hundred different ways, for example by breaking one of the taboos associated with them, but one can choose neither to initiate nor to terminate a relationship with them. We are all irrevocably born into such relationships, which can therefore never be made the object of an inner decision. Secondary religious experience, however, has its roots in a revelation that cannot be seen or experienced, but that must simply be believed in "with all thine heart, and with all thy soul, and with all thy might." In this detachment from the sensuous world lies what Sigmund Freud called "progress in intellectuality," which is to be considered one of the most fundamental characteristics of secondary religious experience.

One important aspect of this new concept and consciousness of sin relates to the exclusiveness of the monotheistic relationship between the divine and the human. In turning to face the world, the One and Only God finds no other partner than the people who believe in him and the human heart that yearns for him, since the world itself is bereft of all godliness. In other words, man bears the full weight of god's address to the world, which is circumscribed in diverse models and metaphors as the loving relationship between groom and bride, as the special bond between a father and his son, a shepherd and his flock, a gardener and his vineyard, and above all—but this is no longer a metaphor—between a ruler and his allies. Never before had man borne such a heavy responsibility towards a contractual partner. The gods of polytheistic religions realized the forms in which they addressed the world in mutual obligations and constellations. In monotheism, the One God invests himself for the first time exclusively in humans and their capacity for love and fidelity. The correlate of this shift is an entirely new sense of inadequacy on the part of humans. The singularity and oneness of the monotheistic god also signifies isolation and solitude. Egyptian texts emphasize this aspect when they call god not just the One, but also the "Lonesome One," who, as Iamblichus transcribes this formula, "tarries in the solitude of his oneness."[20] That is first of all the primal god *before* the creation or genesis of the world, and later the creator and sun god *in* the created or arisen world, insofar as he can be thought of not only as dwelling within the world, but as standing outside it as well. Yet this god, since he does not enter into a covenant with man, can only be experienced in the world by manifesting himself in the differentiated multiplicity of a divine world. The biblical god is solitary and lonesome even in the forms in which he addresses the world, and thus in a much more radical sense. He therefore relies on human love and fidelity. In his Joseph novels, Thomas Mann draws the closest possible connection between god's isolation and his jealousy: "Yes, God too, the Lord, was lonely in His greatness; and Joseph's blood and his memory spoke in the realization that the isolation of a wifeless and childless God had much to do with the jealousy of the bond He had made with man."[21]

The other aspect of the specifically monotheistic concept of sin is idolatry, that is, succumbing to the temptation to worship false gods. The commandment to renounce false gods evidently meets with the greatest resistance in the human soul. Such resistance is repeatedly thematized in the Bible. It is not easy for man to tear himself away from gods declared to be false. For these gods enjoy the advantage and attraction of natural evidence, which is precisely what revealed truth lacks. The gods of this world tenaciously defend the divinity of that world, which is radically disenchanted by monotheistic religion. The biblical texts are full of this resistance.

The thesis that a new kind of guilt came into the world with the Mosaic distinction, and with it a new concept of guilt, was attacked with especial severity by my critics. Gerhard Kaiser, in particular, took offense at the "somber tones" in which I painted monotheism.[22] Yet these "somber tones" are the primary colors on the palette of monotheistic religion. Incidentally, I am not claiming that "sin and guilt are the result of the division of the world through the Mosaic distinction," merely that a new consciousness and conception of guilt came into the world with this distinction and the turn it brought about in the history of consciousness. This assertion does not imply any value judgment. In my eyes, the development of a refined and deepened consciousness of guilt represents a civilizational high-point, the biblical equivalent to the discovery of the tragic in ancient Greece. The invention of sin is a part of "progress in intellectuality," for "it takes understanding to sin; yes, at bottom, all spirit is nothing else than understanding of sin."[23]

Conclusion

"Whoever discovers god in Egypt cancels this distinction"—the German edition of my book on *Moses the Egyptian* ends with this sentence, and I cannot take it amiss of my readers if they took it to mean that I thought to have discovered god in Egypt and dreamed of doing away with the Mosaic distinction. Suffice to say that I have not discovered god in Egypt; indeed, I generally set little store by the arguments for god's existence familiar from religious history. Nor do I dream of doing away with the Mosaic distinction. What I wanted to say with this sentence was that all those who turned Moses into an Egyptian and claimed to have discovered "god in Egypt," from Spencer to Schiller (and all the way up to Freud, although I no longer hold to this genealogy today), were out to cancel the Mosaic distinction. I was concerned with the mnemohistorical logic of the Moses debate: who is telling the story, how is it being told, and with what underlying intentions?

When I, for my part, revisited this story in *Moses the Egyptian*, I also naturally had to ask myself why I, as a non-Jew, Christian, German, and Egyptologist, was so fascinated by this theme. It probably goes without saying that a German of my generation would take special interest in the problem of anti-Semitism, and as an Egyptologist, I have long been interested in investigating the extent to which the memory of ancient Egypt seeped into the foundations of the self-image of the West and its cultural memory. The Moses myth—if I may so designate the story once it has been divested of its undeniable yet intangible historical kernel and become a pure figure of memory—calls the Egyptologist on to the scene as well, and not just, as Freud believed, because here an accurate Egyptian historical account was painted over and distorted in the Bible, but because here a particular image of Egypt was codified. Monotheistic religion, to take up Freud's expression, defines itself in the Exodus story by differentiating itself from Egypt. Egypt had to be left behind so that the promised land of monotheism could be reached. I do not wish to rule out the possibility that this version of events could be true in a historical sense; at any rate, it is symbolically true, and I must confess to finding the symbolic truth more interesting than the possible historical truth, namely, that a group of Hebrew nomads or guest-workers perhaps really did leave Egypt under the leadership of a man who bore the Egyptian name of Moses.

As for the psychohistorical consequences of monotheism, what matters is not so much what really took place but how it was remembered and why it was considered worth telling. In this sense, I agree with Freud in finding it quite remarkable that the name Moses is Egyptian, that the narrative strongly emphasizes that Moses was brought up in the Egyptian court as a prince, that "the man Moses enjoyed great authority in the land of Egypt," and hence that in returning to his people, he had to change his identity. Monotheism requires conversion, first on a personal and then on a collective level. When god says, "I have called my son out of Egypt," what is meant by "Egypt" is not just a geographical space but a self-contained spiritual world. Egypt stands symbolically for a general relationship to the world and to god, including the "spirituality" associated with it, from which one must set forth, or as the Bible says, "be drawn out." Humankind would never have progressed to monotheism in the natural course of events, in the sense of a gradual evolution. Monotheism demands emigration, delimitation, conversion, revolution, a radical turning towards the new resulting from an equally radical break, abnegation, and denial of the old.

The decisive moments of monotheism are accordingly situations of conversion. The Hebrews in thrall to pagan idolatry are converted to monotheism by Moses, Paul converts Jews and Gentiles to Christianity, Mohammed converts Jews, Christians, and infidels to Islam; and in all these situations of conversion, the Mosaic distinction between true and false is reintroduced and tightened. The Mosaic distinction must constantly be drawn anew. There can be no doubt that the Third Reich numbers among these "historical crisis situations in which the 'Mosaic distinction' became vitally important," as Karl-Josef Kuschel has remarked.[1] Confronted with this tyrannical regime, both Sigmund Freud and Thomas Mann interpreted monotheism as "progress in intellectuality," albeit with reference to the irrevocable foundations of humanity rather than to any god-given revelation. I agree entirely with Kuschel when he writes that "the experience of catastrophe forced the Mosaic distinction."[2] It forced it no less for Heinrich Heine than it did for Sigmund Freud and Thomas Mann.

The Moses myth draws a border and strikes a distinction: the distinction between Egypt and Israel, between the old relationship to the world and the new, between the other gods and the one true god, between truth and falsehood in religion and, in the final instance, between god and the world. This distinction has stamped the Jewish as well as the Christian and Islamic soul with its psychohistorical consequences. In my view, it is completely irrelevant whether a religion worships angels and saints alongside the one true god, and even the figures of the son and the holy spirit still do not make Christianity anything like polytheism. Of far greater importance is the border beyond which there are other gods, false gods, idols, superstition, magic, heresies, and all other possible forms of religious "untruth." Wherever this borderline is drawn, we are dealing with the new religion and its psychohistorical consequences. It goes without saying that Christianity and Islam draw this border as well as Judaism. The sole difference lies in the fact that Judaism draws it to exclude itself, whereas the other monotheisms draw it to exclude others. By worshipping the one true god, the Jews isolate themselves from the peoples, who are of no further interest to them. Through their strict adherence to the laws, they cultivate a life-form in which this voluntary isolation finds symbolic expression. Christianity made it its mission to put an end to this self-imposed isolation and open itself to all peoples. Now everything and everyone is excluded that refuses to take up this invitation. Monotheism thereby became invasive, at the very least, and occasionally aggressive as well. The same holds true for Islam, which redefines the borderline in political terms and distinguishes, not just between true and false, but likewise between subjugation and warfare (the dar al-Islam and dar al-Harb) in religion. In each case, monotheism defines itself with reference to an opposite that it excludes as paganism.

What I believe to have discovered in Egypt is the repressed and forgotten side of monotheism, the dark side of monotheism, so to speak, which has remained present in the cultural memory of the West as an object of negation and denial at best. That we are dealing here with a case of "repression" in the classical (that is, Freudian) sense can be deduced from the eruptive forcefulness with which this repressed dark side has continually returned to haunt the West: in the idea of a *prisca theologia* and in Renaissance hermeticism, in the ideas of natural religion, Spinozism, and pantheism in the Enlightenment and early Romanticism, and in the various neo-cosmotheisms, from the Munich cosmicists through to "Hitler's god,"[3] the Wicca cult, and other New Age religious fads.[4]

I am thus endeavoring to undertake a labor of remembrance that brings the repressed to light so that it may then be worked through or "sublimated," to borrow Freud's expression. I want to sublimate the Mosaic distinction, not revoke it. I firmly believe, notwithstanding Karl-Josef Kuschel's objections, that we can no longer rely on "absolute" truths, only on relative, pragmatic truths, which will constantly need to be renegotiated. The Mosaic distinction stands, as Freud has taught us, not just for trauma, repression, and neurosis, but equally for a "progress in intellectuality," which ought not to be relinquished, no matter how dearly it may have been purchased. We need to hold fast to the distinction between true and false, to clear concepts of what we feel to be irreconcilable with our convictions, if these convictions are to retain their strength and depth. But we will no longer be able to ground this distinction in revelations that have been given once and for all. In this way, we must make the Mosaic distinction the object of incessant reflection and redefinition, subjecting it to a "discursive fluidification" (Jürgen Habermas), if it is to remain, for us, the indispensable basis for an advance in humanity.

Notes

INTRODUCTION

1. Theo Sundermeier, "Religion, Religions," in *Dictionary of Mission: Theology, History, Perspectives*, ed. K. Müller et al. (Maryknoll, N.Y., 1997), 387–97; cf. also Sundermeier, *Was ist Religion? Religionswissenschaft im theologischen Kontext* (Gütersloh, 1999).

2. Karl Jaspers, *Vom Ursprung und Ziel der Geschichte* (Munich, 1949); see also Aleida Assmann, "Einheit und Vielheit in der Geschichte: Jaspers' Achsenzeit-Konzept, neu betrachtet," in *Kulturen der Achsenzeit*, ed. Schmuel Eisenstadt, 2, *Indien* (Frankfurt, 1992), 3: 330ff., and id., "Jaspers' Achsenzeit, oder Schwierigkeiten mit der Zentralperspektive in der Geschichte," in *Karl Jaspers: Denken zwischen Wissenschaft, Politik und Philosophie*, ed. D. Harth (Stuttgart, 1989), 187–205.

3. Jaspers's axial age theorem has a long prehistory, which incidentally is neglected in his book itself. That book is based on observations and reflections that date back to the eighteenth century. The French Persian scholar A.-H. Anquetil-Duperron, discoverer of the Zend-Avesta, had already remarked on the simultaneity and unidirectionality of transformational processes in religion from China to Greece in the first century BCE, speaking of a "grande revolution du genre humain" (D. Metzler, "A. H. Anquetil-Duperron (1731–1805) und das Konzept der Achsenzeit," in *Achaemenid History* 7 [1991]: 123–33). In the twentieth century, this notion of a (near-)global spiritual turning was taken up, prior to Jaspers, by Alfred Weber in *Kultursoziologie* (Amsterdam, 1935), and, after Jaspers, above all by Eric Voegelin, in *Order and History*, 5 vols. (Baton Rouge, 1956–87), esp. vol. 1, *Israel and Revelation*. The most important volume came out in 1975 under the felicitous title *The Age of Transcendence*, and the debate continued in the 1970s in the American journal *Daedalus*. Since then, a circle around Schmuel Eisenstadt and Johann Arnason has pursued these problems at a number of conferences, the proceedings of which have appeared in a series of edited volumes: *The Origins and Diversity of Axial Civilizations*, ed. S. N. Eisenstadt (Albany, N.Y., 1986); *Kulturen der Achsenzeit II: Ihre institutionelle und kulturelle Dynamik*, 3 vols. (Frankfurt, 1992); *Axial Civilizations and World History*, ed. Johann P. Arnason, S.

N. Eisenstadt, and Björn Wittrock, Jerusalem Studies in Religion and Culture 4 (Leiden, 2005), as have the proceedings of the conferences organized by Wolfgang Schluchter on Max Weber's theories of the progressive disenchantment and rationalization of the world (for a summary, see W. Schluchter, *Religion und Lebensführung*, 2 vols. [Frankfurt, 1988]). As an Egyptologist, I have sought to link up with these research projects—not just in *Moses the Egyptian*, but already in *Ma'at* (1990) and *Das kulturelle Gedächtnis* (1992)—and I regard the "great revolution of the human race" spoken of by Anquetil-Duperron from the viewpoint of a culture that preceded that shift.

4. See Jan Assmann, *Moses der Ägypter: Entzifferung einer Gedächtnisspur* (Munich, 1998), trans. as *Moses the Egyptian: The Memory of Egypt in Western Monotheism* (Cambridge, Mass., 1997).

5. [Ralf Rendtorff, "Ägypten und die 'Mosaische Unterscheidung'," in Jan Assmann, *Die Mosaische Unterscheidung oder Der Preis des Monotheismus* (Munich, 2003), 201. This quotation, like the four that immediately follow it, is taken from an essay reprinted as an appendix to the German edition of the book.—Trans.]

6. [Klaus Koch, "Monotheismus als Sündenbock," in Assmann, *Mosaische Unterscheidung*, 233–34.—Trans.]

7. [Erich Zenger, "Was ist der Preis des Monotheismus?" in Assmann, *Mosaische Unterscheidung*, 210.—Trans.]

8. [Karl-Josef Kuchel, "Moses, Monotheismus und die Kultur der Moderne," in Assmann, *Mosaische Unterscheidung*, 274.—Trans.]

9. [Zenger, "Was ist der Preis des Monotheismus?" 214.—Trans.] "By recalling the original unity of the Egyptians' tolerant nature-monotheism, Assmann hopes to offer an alternative to the evil consequences of the intolerant monotheism of Moses, Jesus, and Mohammed and the three religions of revelation," according to Willi Oelmüller, *Negative Theologie heute: Die Lage des Menschen vor Gott* (Munich, 1999), 16–17. But I spoke of "cosmotheism," by which I mean polytheism, not "nature-monotheism."

CHAPTER 1

1. Gerhard von Rad, *Theologie des Alten Testaments* (Munich, 1957), 1: 231.

2. Bernhard Lang, *Jahwe der biblische Gott: Ein Porträt* (Munich, 2002).

3. I would like at this point to thank my friends Horst Folkers (Freiburg) and Gert Schröder (Stuttgart). One drew my attention to this parallel case at a discussion of my theses with Gerhard Kaiser in Hinterzarten (November 2000), the other developed the concept of an "Aristotelian distinction" at a conference in June 2002, a concept that pointed in the same direction and greatly encouraged me to elaborate my ideas here.

4. Werner Jäger, *Paideia: The Ideals of Greek Culture*, trans. Gilbert Highet, vol. 1 (Oxford, 1954), 175; translation modified. See also id., *Die Theologie der frühen griechischen Denker* (Darmstadt, 1964), 112–26. The Berlin philosopher of religion Klaus Heinrich has investigated the distinction introduced by Parmenides in several publications. See in particular his *Versuch über die Schwierigkeit, nein zu sagen* (Frankfurt, 1964); *Parmenides und Jona* (Frankfurt, 1982); and *Tertium Datur: Eine religionsphilosophische Einführung in die Logik* (Frankfurt, 1987), 39–50.

5. Claude Lévi-Strauss, *La pensée sauvage* (Paris, 1962).

6. David Hume, *The Natural History of Religions* (1757), esp. chap. 9, "Comparison of these Religions [i.e., polytheism and monotheism] with Regard to Persecution and Toleration." I use the edition of his *Writings on Religion*, ed. Antony Flew (La Salle, Ill., 1992), 145–48.

7. This position is imputed to me, e.g., by Regina M. Schwartz, *The Curse of Cain: The Violent Legacy of Monotheism* (Chicago, 1997).

8. Koch, "Monotheismus als Sündenbock?" in Assmann, *Mosaische Unterscheidung*, 229–30.

9. Zenger, "Was ist der Preis des Monotheismus?" in Assmann, *Mosaische Unterscheidung*, 216.

10. H. Zirker, "Monotheismus und Intoleranz," in *Mit den Anderen leben: Wege zur Toleranz*, ed. K. Hilpert and J. Werbick (Düsseldorf, 1995), 95–117, quotation from pp. 95–96.

11. Eric Santner, *On the Psychotheology of Everyday Life: Reflections on Freud and Rosenzweig* (Chicago, 2001), who discusses *Moses the Egyptian* on pp. 3–6, distinguishes between "global" and "universal consciousness," assigning polytheistic translatability to the "global" option and monotheism's relation to humankind to the "universal" option. Santner's argument is that, by estranging me to myself or disclosing the stranger within me, monotheism (like psychoanalysis) opens me up to the stranger. If we replace the word "stranger" with "pagan," we come a little closer to the truth. After all, what "strangeness" means here is first determined by monotheism. By denouncing the pagan within me, monotheism opens my eyes to "the pagans." Self-hate and hatred for others intermesh, and hatred for others is no less menacing for having its roots in self-hate.

12. While it is true that Judaism did not endorse an evangelical mission, it attracted a great many proselytes by its example. See Rodney Stark, *One True God: Historical Consequences of Monotheism* (Princeton, 2001), 52–59.

13. See Jan Assmann, "Gottes willige Vollstrecker: Zur politischen Theologie der Gewalt," *Saeculum* 51 (2000): 161–74, in which I deal mainly with Egyptian and Assyrian theologies of violence.

14. See Richard A. Litke, *A Reconstruction of the Assyro-Babylonian God-Lists, AN: Anu-um and AN: Anu _a Am_li*, Yale Babylonian Collection, 3 (New Haven,

1998); W. G. Lambert, "Götterlisten," in *Reallexikon der Assyriologie* (1957–71), 3: 473–79.

15. U. Duchrow sees this as evidence of the translatability of the monotheistic religion as well.

16. Augustine *De consensu evangelistarum* 1.22.30 and 23.31, *PL* 34, 1005–6 = Varro fr. 1, 58b; see also Martin Hengel, *Judentum und Hellenismus*, 3rd ed. (Tübingen, 1988), 472n19 and 477n33.

17. Celsus *ap.* Origen *Contra Celsum* 1.24, 5.41 (45); see also Hengel, *Judentum und Hellenismus*, 476.

18. On this, see Assmann, *Moses the Egyptian*, 245n89.

19. I thank Almut Sh. Bruckstein for explaining this passage to me.

20. See Sigmund Freud, *Moses and Monotheism*, trans. James Strachey, in *The Origins of Religion* (Harmondsworth, UK, 1986).

21. See, e.g., Schwartz, *Curse of Cain* (cited n. 7 above).

22. On the problem of interreligious hermeneutics, see Theo Sundermeier, *Den Fremden verstehen* (Göttingen, 1996).

23. See Georges Devereux, "Antagonistic Acculturation," *American Sociological Review* 7 (1943): 133–47. I. Eibl-Eibesfeldt, *Krieg und Frieden aus der Sicht der Verhaltensforschung* (Munich, 1975), does not distinguish between otherness and antagonism. The factors of internal group formation ("love") produce not just otherness, but hostility as well ("hate") when directed outwards. No group can gain inner coherence without hating the other. I take this construction, which strongly recalls Carl Schmitt and the concept of the "political" he derives from the friend/ foe distinction, to be reductionistic. Enmity is a special case of otherness, and otherness is always to be seen in connection with processes of "translation."

24. See Jan Assmann, "In Bilder verstrickt: Bildkult, Idolatrie und Kosmotheismus in der Antike," in *Metapher und Wirklichkeit: Die Logik der Bildhaftigkeit im Reden von Gott, Mensch und Natur*, ed. Reinhold Bernhardt and Ulrike Link-Wieczorek (Göttingen, 1999), 73–88.

25. On these and other texts, see Angelika Berlejung, *Die Theologie der Bilder: Herstellung und Einweihung von Kultbildern in Mesopotamien und die alttestamentliche Bildpolemik*, Orbis biblicus et orientalis 162 (Fribourg, 1998), 369–411.

26. On this genre, see Peter Seibert, *Die Charakteristik: Untersuchungen zu einer altägyptischen Sprechsitte und ihren literarischen Ausprägungen* (Wiesbaden, 1967).

27. See Jan Assmann, "Semiosis and Interpretation in Ancient Egyptian Ritual," in *Interpretation in Religion* (Philosophy and Religion 2), ed. S. Biderman and B.-A. Scharfstein (Leiden, 1992), 87–110.

28. See Hengel, *Judentum und Hellenismus*.

CHAPTER 2

1. Ralph Cudworth, *The True Intellectual System of the Universe, 1678* (New York, 1978); see also Assmann, *Moses the Egyptian,* 79–90.

2. Assmann, *Moses the Egyptian,* 168–207.

3. See *Religionsgeschichte Israels oder Theologie des alten Testaments?* ed. B. Janowski, N. Lohfink, et al., *Jahrbuch für Biblische Theologie* (Neukirchen-Vluyn) 10 (1995); *Religionsgeschichte Israels: Formale und materiale Aspekte,* ed. B. Janowski and M. Köckert (Gütersloh, 1999); O. Keel, "Religionsgeschichte Israels oder Theologie des Alten Testaments?" in *Wieviel Systematik erlaubt die Schrift? Auf der Suche nach einer gesamtbiblischen Theologie,* ed. F. L. Hossfeld (Freiburg, 2001), 88–109. Following Rainer Albertz, *Religionsgeschichte Israels in alttestamentlicher Zeit,* 2 vols. (Göttingen, 1992), the issue of "theology or history of religion" has generated controversy in Old Testament studies, but the category of the Mosaic distinction allows us to resolve it in the sense of "both . . . and." With the Mosaic distinction and the introduction of an exclusive concept of truth, a gap opens up between normative-systematic demands and religious practice.

4. Morton Smith, *Palestinian Parties and Politics That Shaped the Old Testament* (New York, 1971); Bernhard Lang, *Der Einzige Gott: Die Geburt des biblischen Monotheismus* (Munich, 1981).

5. See Jan Assmann, "Zoroaster/Zarathustra in der Gedächtnis- und Forschungsgeschichte des Abendlandes," in *Archiv für Religionsgeschichte* 3 (Leipzig, 2001), 308–15.

6. In his book *Weltbilder der Religionen* (Zurich, 2001), the Swiss scholar of religion Fritz Stolz characterizes monotheism as distinguishing between "god and the world" (139–212).

7. The thesis that one only recognizes a truth when one understands what it excludes as untrue naturally holds only in a cultural and scientific sense, and not in a theological one. Karl Barth would certainly not have subscribed to it. Then it would only be a relative rather than an absolute truth. I would therefore like to emphasize once again that I am approaching this theme as a cultural scientist, not as a theologian. I am studying revolutionary monotheism as a historical phenomenon and as a particular cultural semantics, which I want to illuminate from its context, and since, in my eyes, we are dealing here with a strongly polemical, antagonistic semantics, I think we can only grasp its meaning as historians and cultural scientists by looking at what it excludes as its opposite. Cultural scientists are methodical relativists, regardless of whatever they may happen to believe outside their professional lives.

8. In these three dimensions, one can discern without difficulty the triad of "theologies" distinguished by Varro in his *Antiquitates rerum divinarum*: the "natural theology" (*theologia naturalis*: cosmic dimension) of the philosophers, the

"poetic theology" (*theologia fabularis*: mythic dimension) of the poets, and the "political theology" (*theologia civilis*: political dimension) of the priests and citizens. See Godo Lieberg, "Die 'theologia tripertita' in Forschung und Bezeugung," *Aufstieg und Niedergang der römischen Welt* 1.4 (1973): 63–115; id., "Die *theologia tripertita* als Formprinzip antiken Denkens," *Rheinisches Museum für Philologie* 125 (1982): 25–52; A. Dihle, "Die *theologia tripertita* bei Augustin," in *Geschichte—Tradition—Reflexion: Festschrift für Martin Hengel zum 70. Geburtstag*, ed. H. Cancik et al., vol. 2 (Tübingen, 1996), 183–202. The missing dimension here is history. Precisely this dimension is foregrounded by monotheism. That is one of the central theses of Martin Buber's *Moses* (Zurich, 1948), and now also of Rodney Stark's *One True God: Historical Consequences of Monotheism* (Princeton, 2001) (I thank Ulrich Nolte for drawing my attention to this book).

9. Rolf Rendtorff objects to the sentence: "Egypt is the maternal body from which the chosen people went forth, but the umbilical cord has been cut once and for all by the Mosaic distinction" (*Moses der Ägypter*, 247). He docs not know what to make of "the metaphor of the maternal body in this context" (Rendtorff, "Ägypten und die 'Mosaische Unterscheidung'," in Assmann, *Mosaische Unterscheidung*, 204). I am referring to Deut. 4:34, where it is said that god removed Israel, "a nation from the midst of another nation," *goj mi-qereb goj*. The Hebrew word *qereb* is very strong; it can also mean "entrails," "the mother's womb."

10. Assmann, *Moses der Ägypter*, 63.

11. Erich Zenger, "Was ist der Preis des Monotheismus?" in Assmann, *Mosaische Unterscheidung*, 217.

12. In *Les deux sources de la morale et de la religion* (Paris, 1932), Henri Bergson introduces the distinction between "religions statiques" and "religions dynamiques," which approximately corresponds to my distinction between religions that immerse themselves in the world (or "conciliatory religions," in Theo Sundermeier's terminology) and religions that distance themselves from it (or redemptive religions).

13. Jürgen Manemann, "Götterdämmerung: Politischer Antimonotheismus in Wendezeiten," in *Monotheismus*, ed. id. et al., *Jahrbuch Politische Theologie* 4 (Münster, 2002): 28–49, quotation from p. 46.

14. H. Stein, *Moses und die Offenbarung der Demokratie* (Berlin, 1998), 29.

15. *Merikare* P 128–30. A. Volten, *Zwei Altägyptische Politische Schriften: Die Lehre für König Merikare und die Lehre des Königs Amenemhet*, Analecta Aegyptiaca 4 (Copenhagen, 1945), 68.

16. See Jan Assmann, *Herrschaft und Heil: Politische Theologie in Altägypten, Israel und Europa* (Munich, 2000). This book was conceived historically, not mnemohistorically. It therefore arrived at quite different conclusions to *Moses the Egyptian*.

17. See N. Lohfink, "Der Begriff des Gottesreichs vom Alten Testament her gesehen," in *Unterwegs zur Kirche: Alttestamentliche Konzeptionen*, ed. J. Schreiner et al., *Quaestiones disputatae* 110 (1987): 33–86, 33–86, esp. p. 44. Lohfink applies the concept of "contrast society" to early Israel in another study as well: "Der gewaltige Gott des Alten Testaments," in *Der eine Gott der beiden Testamente, Jahrbuch für Biblische Theologie* (Neukirchen) 2 (1987): 106–36, esp. 119–36.

18. M. Sandman, *Texts from the Time of Akhenaten*, Bibliotheca Aegyptica 8 (Brussels, 1938), 86.15–16.

19. *Gerechtigkeit: Richten und Retten in der abendländischen Tradition und ihren altorientalischen Ursprüngen*, ed. Jan Assmann, Bernd Janowski, and Michael Welker (Munich, 1998); B. Janowski, *Die rettende Gerechtigkeit* (Neukirchen-Vluyn, 1999).

20. See Jan Assmann, *Egyptian Solar Religion in the New Kingdom* (London, 1995), 30–37.

21. See Jan Assmann, *Ma'at: Gerechtigkeit und Unsterblichkeit im Alten Ägypten* (Munich, 1990).

22. The most recent English translation is to be found in R. Parkinson, *The Tale of Sinuhe and Other Ancient Egyptian Poems* (Oxford, 1997). On the interpretation of this text, see *Reading the Eloquent Peasant: Proceedings of the International Conference on The Tale of the Eloquent Peasant at the University of California, Los Angeles, March 27–30, 1997*, ed. A. Gnirs, Lingua Aegyptia 8 (Göttingen, 2000).

23. Bergson, *Les deux sources de la morale et de la religion*.

24. Most recently, with great forcefulness and with reference to her numerous precursors, by Miriam Lichtheim, *Moral Values in Ancient Egypt*, Orbis biblicus et orientalis 155 (Fribourg, 1997), 89–99.

25. E. Otto, *Wesen und Wandel der ägyptischen Kultur* (Heidelberg, 1969), 60.

26. Lichtheim, *Moral Values*, 89.

27. Pierre Bayle, "Pensées diverses à l'occasion de la comète" (1682), in *Oeuvres diverses*, vol. 3 (Den Haag, 1727), 9ff. See also W. Schröder, *Ursprünge des Atheismus: Untersuchungen zur Metaphysik- und Religionskritik des 17. und 18. Jahrhunderts*, Questiones, 11 (Stuttgart, 1998), 68–69.

28. See *Moral und Weltreligionen*, ed. Christof Gestrich, *Berliner theologische Zeitschrift* suppl. vol. (Berlin, 2000), 129–70.

29. [In 2000, the philosopher Peter Sloterdijk delivered a speech entitled "Rules for the Human Park" that was widely condemned for supposedly advocating a eugenics program reminiscent of the Nazi policy of "racial hygiene."—Trans.]

30. See Jan Assmann, "Religion und Gerechtigkeit," in *Gerechtigkeit heute: Anspruch und Wirklichkeit*, ed. Heinrich Schmidinger, Salzburger Hochschulwochen 2000 (Vienna, 2000), 13–30.

31. Friedrich Nietzsche, *On the Genealogy of Morals*, trans. Douglas Smith (Oxford, 1996), 11–38.

128   *Notes*

32. In his study on ancient Judaism, Max Weber enthusiastically adopted the theory of *ressentiment*. See E. Fleischmann, "Max Weber, die Juden und das Ressentiment," in *Max Webers Studie über das antike Judentum*, ed. W. Schluchter (Frankfurt, 1981), 263–86.

33. See Assmann, *Ma'at*, 273–78.

34. See Assmann, *Herrschaft und Heil*, 46–52.

35. For examples of this transfer process, see ibid.

36. See Diethard Römheld, *Wege der Weisheit: Die Lehren Amenemopes und Proverbien 22, 17–24, 12* (Berlin, 1989).

37. See the excellent anthology compiled by Hellmut Brunner, *Altägyptische Weisheit* (Zurich, 1988).

38. See Assmann, *Ma'at*.

39. See, e.g., Gerhard von Rad, *Weisheit in Israel* (Neukirchen, 1970); Bernhard Lang, "Klugheit als Ethos und Weisheit als Beruf: Zur Lebenslehre im Alten Testament," in *Weisheit*, ed. Aleida Assmann (Munich, 1991), 177–92.

40. See Römheld, *Wege der Weisheit*.

41. See Jan Assmann, *Ägypten: Eine Sinngeschichte* (Munich, 1996), 178–95; id., *Ma'at*, chap. 5; and *Gerechtigkeit*, ed. id. et al.

42. *Book of the Dead*, chap. 125; see Erik Hornung, *Das Totenbuch der Ägypter* (Zurich, 1979), 233–45.

CHAPTER 3

1. Along with Gerhard Kaiser, see also Franz Maciejewski, "Ausschließlichkeitsansprüche in der Holocaustdebatte," in *Kritik und Geschichte der Intoleranz*, ed. R. Kloepfer and B. Dücker (Heidelberg, 2000), 199–214, here 204–8. Maciejewski denies any connection between the legend of the lepers as related by Manetho and the Amarna period. In his opinion, it is a question here of hatred for the Jews rather than "antimonotheism."

2. I think it nonetheless feasible that Psalm 104 originated in a Babylonian translation of the Great Hymn that was brought to Canaan with diplomatic correspondence and subsequently assimilated into the local poetic tradition.

3. Cf. also Ernst Baltrusch, "Bewunderung, Duldung, Ablehnung: Das Urteil über die Juden in der griechisch-römischen Literatur," *KLIO* 80 (1998): 403–21.

4. Peter Schäfer, *Judeophobia: Attitudes Toward the Jews in the Ancient World* (Cambridge, Mass., 1997).

5. Zvi Yavetz, *Judenfeindschaft in der Antike* (Munich, 1996). See also Ernst Baltrusch, *Die Juden und das Römische Reich: Geschichte einer konfliktreichen Beziehung* (Darmstadt, 2002).

6. Amos Funkenstein, *Perceptions of Jewish History* (Berkeley, 1993), 32–49.

7. Babylonian Talmud, Sabbat 89a.

8. See also Antonio Loprieno, *La pensée et l'écriture* (Paris, 2002), 110–15. My interpretation of Manetho's report as a memory of the Amarna period has been widely accepted in Egyptological circles, alongside other memories like those of the Hyksos, the Assyrians, and the Persians.

9. Maciejewski, "Ausschließlichkeitsansprüche." In his recent book *Psychoanalytisches Archiv und jüdisches Gedächtnis: Freud, Beschneidung und Monotheismus* (Vienna, 2002), 293–307, Maciejewski corrects his interpretation on this point in response to an earlier version of this chapter, "Antijudaismus oder Antimonotheismus? Hellenistische Exoduserzählungen," which appeared in *Das Judentum im Spiegel seiner kulturellen Umwelten*, ed. Dieter Borchmeyer and Helmuth Kiesel (Neckargemünd, 2002), 33–54.

10. Eduard Meyer, *Aegyptische Chronologie* (Leipzig, 1904), 92–95; Rolf Krauss, *Das Ende der Amarna-Zeit* (Hildesheim, 1978). Donald B. Redford traces the legend of the lepers back to the Amarna period in his article "The Hyksos Invasion in History and Tradition," *Orientalia* 39 (1970): 1–51, as well as in his book *Pharaonic King Lists, Annals and Day-Books: A Contribution to the Study of the Egyptian Sense of History* (Mississauga, Ontario, 1986), 293.

11. See Hans Goedicke, "The 'Canaanite' Illness," *Studien zur Altägyptischen Kultur* 11 (1984): 91–105, and id., "The End of the Hyksos in Egypt," in *Egyptological Studies in Honor of Richard A. Parker*, ed. Leonard L. Lesko (Hanover, N.H., 1986), 37–47.

12. On leprosy in ancient Egypt, see W. Westendorf, "Die Lepra im pharaonischen Ägypten," in *Aussatz—Lepra—Hansen-Krankheit. Ein Menschheitsproblem im Wandel*, ed. J. H. Wolf (Würzburg, 1986), 35–57; Th. Bardinet, "Remarques sur les maladies de la peau, la lèpre et le châtiment divin dans l'Égypte ancienne," *Revue d'Égyptologie 39* (1988) : 3–36.

13. Like the high priests in Israel, the Sakhmet priests in Egypt were charged with keeping leprosy under control. According to information provided by J. F. Quack, the "Book of the Temple" dictates that the Sakhmet priest banish lepers from the city: "He is the one who inspects all the people to keep the *Hemut-Sa* sickness outside the city, to prevent it from coming any closer, and to purify the places where it is found; he assumes responsibility for the *Wemha* sickness, leprosy, the *mesheshut* sickness, the *shememet* inflammation of the skin, the *serfet* inflammation, stroke and the *peschit* sickness." Mary Douglas detected a parallel in the way lepers and idolaters are treated in the Book of Numbers; much the same holds true in Egyptian semantics. See Mary Douglas, "In the Wilderness: The Doctrine of Defilement in the Book of Numbers," *Journal for the Study of the Old Testament*, suppl. ser., 158 (Sheffield, 1993): 148.

14. A. I. Elanskaya and O. D. Berlev, "*nshelket* in *Apophthegmata patrum* and *hoi lelobemenoi* in Manetho," in *Coptology—Past, Present, and Future: Studies in Honour of Rodolphe Kasser*, ed. S. Giversen, M. Krause, and P. Nagel, Orientalia

Lovaniensia analecta 61 (1994): 305–16, esp. 309ff., see in the motif of leprosy an allusion to the peculiarities of Amarna art, (mis)understood by later witnesses as signs of physical deformation. Such art was still visible in portraits of Akhenaten and the royal family on the boundary stelae of Amarna. In their opinion, Manetho is the first to have interpreted royal iconography of the Amarna period in terms of illness, namely, leprosy. They bring this into connection with a passage in Artapanos, who said of Chenephres, the pharaoh in whose court Moses was supposedly raised, that he was the first man to have been deformed by elephantiasis (Jacoby, *Die Fragmente der griechischen Historiker III C* [Leiden, 1969], no. 726).

15. A. H. Gardiner, *Journal of Egyptian Archaeology* 32 (1946): 43–56.

16. See also M. Görg, "Der sogenannte Exodus zwischen Erinnerung und Polemik," in *Jerusalem Studies in Egyptology*, Egypt and the Old Testament 40 (1998): 169.

17. *Pap. Harris I* 75, 2–7. Pierre Grandet, *Le papyrus Harris I (BM 9999)*, Bibliothèque d'Étude 109 (Cairo, 1994), 1: 335–36, 2: 215–36, as well as the Elephantine stela of Sethnacht; see S. J. Seidlmeyer, "Epigraphische Bemerkungen zur Stele des Sethnachte aus Elephantine," in *Stationen: Festschrift Stadelmann*, ed. H. Guksch and D. Polz (Mainz, 1998), 384–86.

18. Maciejewski, "Ausschließlichkeitsansprüche," 208.

19. Ibid., 208–9n18. That is to say: I wanted to absolve the Jews of all blame for having invented monotheism. But to make the point once again, I find nothing in monotheism with which to reproach it. Like Maciejewski, I regard the "introduction of monotheism" as "one of the great achievements of Western civilization," and I concur with Freud in seeing monotheism as an "advance in intellectuality."

20. A. H. Gardiner, *The Inscription of Mes: A Contribution to the Study of Egyptian Judicial Procedure*, Untersuchungen zur Geschichte und Altertumskunde Ägyptens 4 (Lepizig, 1903–5), pp. 14, 11, 23, nn. 54 and 82.

21. Maciejewski, *Psychoanalytisches Archiv*, 297.

22. Ibid., 300.

23. On animal worship in Late Period Egypt and its appraisal throughout antiquity, see K. A. D. Smelik and E. A. Hemelrijk, "'Who knows not what monsters demented Egypt worships?' Opinions on Egyptian Animal Worship in Antiquity as Part of the Ancient Conceptions of Egypt," *Aufstieg und Niedergang der römischen Welt* II, 17.4 (Berlin, 1984), 1852–2000, 2337–57.

24. See Jan Assmann, *Monotheismus und Kosmotheismus: Altägyptische Formen des "Denkens des Einen" und ihre abendländische Rezeptionsgeschichte* (Heidelberg, 1993).

25. See Jan Assmann, *Politische Theologie zwischen Ägypten und Israel* (Munich, 1992), 48–63; id., *Herrschaft und Heil: Politische Theologie in Altägypten, Israel und Europa* (Munich, 2000), 37–45. How Ottmar John, "Zur Logik des Monotheismus: Verteidigung des Monotheismus gegen den Vorwurf seiner inhärenten Ge-

walttätigkeit," in *Monotheismus*, ed. Jürgen Manemann et al., *Jahrbuch Politische Theologie* 4 (Münster, 2002), 142–53, can arrive at the idea that polytheisms, as I depict them, are characterized "by an unreflected immediacy to the numinous" (p. 148) is no less baffling than his claim that, for me, "religion is always an act of immediacy between humans and gods, the profane and the sacral" (p. 150). Moreover, I do not see in the ban on graven images a "religious arrogation of political power" (p. 147) but quite the opposite, a blocking of such arrogation. "A fundamental error on Assmann's part," John continues, "is to divorce the ban on graven images from its context. The ban is embedded in the revelation of the law on Sinai." I fail to see where and how I ignored this "context." On the contrary, my principal aim is to contextualize the ban on graven images in history and philology.

26. See Boyo Ockinga, *Die Gottebenbildlichkeit im Alten Ägypten und im Alten Testament*, Ägypten und Altes Testament 7 (Wiesbaden, 1984).

27. On the biblical ban on graven images, see Christoph Dohmen, *Das Bilderverbot: Seine Entstehung und seine Entwicklung im Alten Testament*, Bonner biblische Beiträge 62, 2nd ed. (Frankfurt, 1987); Tryggve N. D. Mettinger, *No Graven Image? Israelite Aniconism in its Near Eastern Context*, Coniectanea Biblica, OT Series 42 (Stockholm, 1995); C. Uehlinger, "Du culte des images à son interdit," *Le Monde de la Bible* 110 (April 1998): 52–63; Angelika Berlejung, *Die Theologie der Bilder: Herstellung und Einweihung von Bildern in Mesopotamien und die alttestamentliche Bilderpolemik*, Orbis biblicus et orientalis 162 (Fribourg, 1998); Michael B. Dick, "Prophetic Parodies of Making the Cult Images," in *Born in Heaven, Made on Earth: The Making of the Cult Image in the Ancient Near East*, ed. id. (Winona Lake, Ind., 1999), 1–54; Rolf Rendtorff, "Was verbietet das alttestamentliche Bilderverbot?" in *Metapher und Wirklichkeit: Die Logik der Bildhaftigkeit im Reden von Gott, Mensch und Natur*, ed. Reinhold Bernhardt and Ulrike Linke-Wieczorek (Göttingen, 1999), 65; Paul M. van Buren, "Idols, Works of Art, and Language, or: What Is Wrong with Graven Images," ibid., 66–72; Jan Assmann, "In Bilder verstrickt. Bildkult, Idolatrie und Kosmotheismus in der Antike," ibid., 73–88; and esp. Othmar Keel, "Warum im Jerusalemer Tempel kein anthropomorphes Kultbild gestanden haben dürfte," in *Homo Pictor*, ed. Gottfried Boehm, Colloquium Rauricum 7 (Munich, 2001), 244–81.

28. Where the ban on graven images is at issue, the Bible does not employ the general world for "image," *selem*, as for example in Gen. 1:26–27 in connection with the divine likeness of humankind, but special terms for "carved image," "cast image," and the like, terms that connote the goal of the operation as the cult image along with the act of production (like our word "fetish," which leads via the Portuguese back to the Latin *facere*, to make or produce).

29. *Asclepius* 24–26, ed. W. Scott, in *Hermetica I* (London, 1968), 341–45; Coptic version: Nag Hammadi Codex VI, 8. 70.3–73.22, ed. M. Krause and P. Labib, "Gnostische und Hermetische Schriften aus Codex II und Codex VI," in *ADAIK*

Koptische Reihe 2 (Glückstadt, 1971), 194–200. C. Colpe and J. Holzhausen, *Das Corpus Hermeticum Deutsch*, Clavis pansophiae 7, 1 (Stuttgart–Bad Cannstadt, 1997), 287–91 (Latin), 540–62 (Coptic). Cf. G. Fowden, *The Egyptian Hermes: A Historical Approach to the Late Pagan Mind* (Cambridge, 1986), 39–43; Jan Assmann, "Königsdogma und Heilserwartung: Politische und kultische Chaosbeschreibungen in ägyptischen Texten," in *Apocalypticism in the Mediterranean World and in the Near East*, ed. D. Hellholm (Tübingen, 1983), 345–77; id., "Magische Weisheit: Wissensformen im ägyptischen Kosmotheimus," in *Stein und Zeit: Mensch und Gesellschaft im Alten Ägypten* (Munich, 1991), 75. J. P. Mahé, *Hermès en Haute-Égypte : Les textes hermétiques de Nag Hammadi et leurs parallèles grecs et latins*, 2 (Quebec, 1982), 69–97; D. Frankfurter, *Elijah in Upper Egypt : The Apocalypse of Elijah and Early Egyptian Christianity* (Minneapolis, 1993), 188–89. The Latin *inrationabilitas bonorum omnium* corresponds to the Coptic "dearth of good words." An end to linguistic comprehension and a growing predominance of violence are among the central motifs of Egyptian descriptions of chaos.

30. See Assmann, *Monotheismus und Kosmotheismus.*

31. *Corpus Hermeticum*, trans. A. J. Festugière, ed. A. D. Nock, 4 vols., Collection Budé (Paris 1945–54); *Hermetica: The Greek Corpus Hermeticum and the Latin Asclepius*, trans. and ed. Brian P. Copenhaver (Cambridge, 1992); *Das Corpus Hermeticum Deutsch: Übersetzung, Darstellung und Kommentierung in drei Teilen*, trans. Jens Holzhausen, ed. Carsten Colpe, Clavis pansophiae 7 (Stuttgart–Bad Cannstatt, 1997).

32. *The Hieroglyphics of Horapollo*, trans. George Boas (Princeton, 1950, repr. 1993); and see also Horapollo, *I geroglifici* (bilingual Greek-Italian edition), ed. Mario Andrea Rigoni and Elena Zanco (Milan 1996).

33. See M. Olender, *Les langages du paradis* (Paris, 1988).

34. "One might say, they are all 'badly christened'; under the thin veneer of Christianity they have remained what their ancestors were, barbarically polytheistic. They have not yet overcome their grudge against the new religion that was forced on them, and they have projected it on to the source from which Christianity came to them. . . . Their hatred for Jews is at bottom hatred for Christianity" (Freud, *Moses and Monotheism*, trans. Katherine Jones [London, 1951], 147–48).

35. Wilhelm Schmidt-Biggemann, *Philosophia Perennis: Historische Umrisse abendländischer Spiritualität in Antike, Mittelalter und Früher Neuzeit* (Frankfurt, 1998).

36. Michael Stausberg, *Faszination Zarathushtra: Zoroaster und die Europäische Religionsgeschichte der Frühen Neuzeit*, Religionsgeschichtliche Versuche und Vorarbeiten 42, 2 vols. (Berlin, 1998).

37. Ibid., 35–82.

38. With reference to Plutarch, *De Iside* 359e.

39. Stausberg, *Faszination Zarathushtra*, 75–76.

40. Scholarios; this is presumably the earliest evidence we have of the concept of "polytheism." On the literature cited by Stausberg, see also *L'impensable polythéisme: Études d'historiographie religieuse*, ed. Francis Schmidt (Paris, 1998).

41. The prototype for this conception appears to be Diodorus Siculus *Bibliotheca historica* 1.94.1–2, which speaks of the six great lawgivers who had identified god as the source of their laws. The first of these, the founder of the Egyptian kingdom, whom Diodorus sometimes calls Menas or Menes, sometimes Mnevis, "claimed that Hermes gave him the laws." Similarly, Minos in Crete referred to Zeus, Lycurgus in Sparta to Apollo, Zoroaster of the "Arians" (*arianoi*) to the *Agathos Daimon* (Ahura Mazda), Zalmoxis of the Getae to Hestia, and Moses of the Jews to *Iao* (Yahweh). Ficino gleans from this passage the model of his "ancient theology" by interpreting the concept of "lawgiving" in the sense of "religion founding." In the eighteenth century, the passage in Diodorus was read very differently, becoming a central point of reference for the radical Enlightenment. From the "six lawgivers," it is then only a small step to the "three tricksters." Ficino understands this passage more in the sense of Diodorus, who seems to have been innocent of any polemical intent.

42. On a typical representative of this ideal, see Anthony Grafton, *Cardano's Cosmos: The Worlds and Works of a Renaissance Astrologer* (Cambridge, Mass., 1999).

43. See Schmidt-Biggemann, *Philosophia Perennis*.

44. Stausberg, *Faszination Zarathushtra*, 288.

45. Ibid., 134.

46. See Aleida Assmann, *Die Legitimität der Fiktion* (Munich, 1980), and "Die Weisheit Adams," in *Weisheit*, ed. id. (Munich, 1991), 305–24.

47. See the book of the same name by Umberto Eco, *The Search for the Perfect Language*, trans. James Fentress (Oxford, 1997).

48. See, e.g., Liselotte Dieckmann, *Hieroglyphics* (Saint Louis, 1970); M. V. David, *Le débat sur les écritures et l'hiéroglyphie aux XVIIe et XVIIIe siècle* (Paris, 1965).

49. These contexts can only be touched on here. For further details, see *Hieroglyphen: Stationen einer anderen abendländischen Grammatologie*, ed. Aleida Assmann and Jan Assmann (Munich, 2003).

50. There is no recent comprehensive study of the Sabians. D. Chwolsohn [D. A. Khvol'son], *Die Ssabier und der Ssabismus*, 2 vols. (St. Petersburg, 1856; repr. New York, 1965), is still indispensable.

51. Sara Stroumsa, "Entre Harrann et al-Maghreb : La théorie maimonidienne de l'histoire des religions et ses sources arabes," in *Judiós y musulmanes en al-Andalus y el Maghreb, contactos intelectuales*, ed. Maribel Fierro (Madrid, 2002), 153–64.

52. Ibn Wahshiyya, *al-filâha al-nabatiyya*, Hebrew *ha-avoda ha-nabatit*. See Toufic Fahd, *L'agriculture nabatéenne: Traduction en arabe attribuée à Abu Bakr Ahmad b. 'Ali al-Kasdani connu sous le nom d'Ibn Wah_iyya (Ive/Ve siècle)* (Damascus, 1998). There is a long discussion in John Spencer's *De legibus Hebraeorum ritualibus et earum rationibus* (1685) on the question of the relationship between "Sabians" (Zabii) and "Sabans" (Sabaei).

53. Stephen Nettles, *Answer to the Jewish Part of Mr Selden's History of Tithes* (Oxford, 1625), 46–47, cited in Guy G. Stroumsa, "John Spencer and the Roots of Idolatry," *History of Religions* 40 (2001): 1–23, p. 17.

54. Stausberg, *Faszination Zarathushtra*, 657ff.

55. Several new publications on Spencer have appeared since *Moses the Egyptian*. See Stroumsa, "John Spencer and the Roots of Idolatry" (cited n. 53 above); Martin Mulsow, *Moderne aus dem Untergrund: Radikale Frühaufklärung in Deutschland, 1680–1720* (Hamburg, 2002), 85–113; Jan Assmann, "Die Historisierung der Religion: Maimonides, Spencer, Schiller, Freud," in *Historicization = Historisierung*, ed. Glenn W. Most, Aporemata: Kritische Studien zur Philologiegeschichte, 5 (Göttingen, 2001), 25–43; Jan Assmann, "Das Geheimnis der Wahrheit: Das Konzept der 'doppelten Religion' und die Erfindung der Religionsgeschichte," in *Archiv für Religionsgeschichte* 3 (Leipzig, 2001), 108–34.

CHAPTER 4

1. See, e.g., Emanuel Rice, *Freud and Moses: The Long Journey Home* (New York, 1990); Ilse Grubrich-Simitis, *Freuds Moses-Studie als Tagtraum* (Weinheim, 1991); Josef Hayim Yerushalmi, *Freud's Moses: Judaism Terminable and Interminable* (New Haven, 1991); Bluma Goldstein, *Reinscribing Moses: Heine, Kafka, Freud, and Schoenberg in a European Wilderness* (Cambridge, Mass., 1992); Robert Paul, *Moses and Civilization: The Meaning behind Freud's Myth* (New Haven, 1996); Jacques Derrida, *Mal d'archive* (Paris, 1995); Richard J. Bernstein, *Freud and the Legacy of Moses* (Cambridge, Mass., 1998); *Sechzig Jahre "Der Mann Moses": Zur Religionskritik von Sigmund Freud*, Wege zum Menschen, special issue, *Monatsschrift für Seelsorge und Beratung* 51, 4 (May–June 1999); Michèle Porte, *Le mythe monothéiste: Une lecture de "L'homme Moïse et la religion monothéiste" de Sigmund Freud* (Fontenay-aux-Roses, 1999); Eric Santner, *On the Psychotheology of Everyday Life: Reflections on Freud and Rosenzweig* (Chicago, 2001); Wolfgang Hegener, *Wege aus der vaterlosen Psychoanalyse: Vier Abhandlungen über Freuds "Mann Moses"* (Tübingen, 2001); Bernd Witte, "Die Schrift im Exil: Sigmund Freuds *Der Mann Moses* und die jüdische Tradition," in *Medialität und Gedächtnis: Interdisziplinäre Beiträge zur kulturellen Verarbeitung kultureller Krisen*, ed. Vittorio Borsò, Gerd Krumeich, and Bernd Witte (Stuttgart, 2001), 55–66; Franz Maciejewski, *Psychoanalytisches Archiv und jüdisches Gedächtnis: Freud, Beschneidung und Monotheis-*

mus (Vienna, 2002). *PSYCHE: Zeitschrift für Psychoanalyse und ihre Anwendungen* 56 (2002) is devoted almost exclusively to Freud's book on Moses.

2. Bernstein cited in preceding note. Bernd Witte also refers to my misreading of Freud in his essay "Die Schrift im Exil," 56–57; I have since retracted it in my article "Der Fortschritt in der Geistigkeit: Freuds Konstruktion des Judentums," *PSYCHE: Zeitschrift für Psychoanalyse und ihre Anwendungen* 56 (2002): 154–71.

3. Sigmund Freud, *Moses and Monotheism*, trans. James Strachey, in *The Origins of Religion* (Harmondsworth, UK, 1986), 237–386.

4. Jacques Derrida, "Violence and Metaphysics: An Essay on the Thought of Emmanuel Levinas," in *Writing and Difference*, trans. Alan Bass (Chicago, 1978), 152.

5. Heinrich Heine, "Ludwig Börne: Eine Denkschrift," in *Werke*, vol. 4 (Frankfurt, 1994), 350. [For an English rendering of this, see *Ludwig Börne: A Memorial*, trans. Jeffrey L. Sammons (Rochester, N.Y., 2006).] This text was written, as Karl-Josef Kuschel has shown, during a period of his life when Heine still opted for the Greek solution; in his last years, he emphatically returned to the "god of our fathers" and the Jewish solution.

6. See H. G. Kippenberg, *Die Entdeckung der Religionsgeschichte: Religionswissenschaft und Moderne* (Munich, 1997), 45–79; Vassili Lambropoulos, *The Rise of Eurocentrism: Anatomy of Interpretation* (Princeton, 1993).

7. M. Olender, *Die Sprachen des Paradieses: Religion, Philologie und Rassentheorie im 19. Jh.* (Frankfurt, 1995).

8. [James Strachey notes in his translation of Freud's *Moses and Monotheism*: "The German word here translated 'intellectuality' is *Geistigkeit* and its rendering raises much difficulty. The obvious alternative would be 'spirituality', but in English this arouses some very different associations" (330n)—Trans.].

9. Freud, *Beyond the Pleasure Principle*, trans. James Strachey (London, 1961), 36. Hegel speaks of an "instinct of the world-spirit" and an "instinct for perfectibility" in his *Vorlesungen zur Philosophie der Geschichte* (Stuttgart, 1961), 104–5.

10. Immanuel Kant, *Critique of the Power of Judgment*, trans. Paul Guyer and Eric Matthews (Cambridge, 2000), 156. Freud explains the feeling of superiority over other religions imparted by monotheism in exactly the same way.

11. Freud, *Moses and Monotheism*, 329–30.

12. *Internationale Zeitschrift für Psychoanalyse und Imago* 24, 1–2 (1939): 6–9.

13. On 2 August 1938. See the editor's note in *Moses and Monotheism*, 239.

14. Here I gratefully follow in the footsteps of Bernstein, *Freud and the Legacy of Moses*, 82–89.

15. Freud, letter to Arnold Zweig, 9 September 1934, in *The Letters of Sigmund Freud and Arnold Zweig*, trans. W. D. Robson-Scott (London, 1970), 91.

16. Freud, *Moses and Monotheism*, 328–29; translation modified.

17. Freud, "The Aetiology of Hysteria," trans. James Strachey, *The Standard Edition of the Complete Psychological Works of Sigmund Freud* (London, 1962), 3: 192. On the archeology metaphor in Freud, see Donald Kuspit, "A Mighty Metaphor: The Analogy of Archaeology and Psychoanalysis," in *Sigmund Freud and Art. His Personal Collection of Antiquities*, ed. Lynn Gamwell and Richard Wells (New York, 1989), 133–51; Karl Stockreiter, "Am Rand der Aufklärungsmetapher: Korrespondenzen zwischen Archäologie und Psychoanalyse," in *"Meine . . . alten und dreckigen Götter": Aus Sigmund Freuds Sammlung*, ed. Lydia Marinelli, catalog of the exhibition in the Sigmund Freud Museum, Vienna, 18 November 1998–17 February 1999 (Basel, 1998), 81–93, and esp. Lydia Flem, *Der Mann Freud* (Frankfurt, 1993), 35–58. On Freud as a collector of antiquities, see also Ana-Maria Rizutto, *Why Did Freud Reject God? A Psychodynamic Interpretation* (New Haven, 1998), 1–21, and *Excavations and Their Objects: Freud's Collection of Antiquities*, ed. Stephen Barker (New York, 1996). See now, too, Richard H. Armstrong, *A Compulsion for Antiquity: Freud and the Ancient World* (Ithaca, N.Y., 2005).

18. Paul Ricoeur, *Freud and Philosophy: An Essay on Interpretation*, trans. Denis Savage (New Haven, 1970).

19. Freud, "Konstruktionen in der Psychoanalyse" (1937), in *Studienausgabe*, suppl. vol. (Frankfurt, 1975), 393–406; *Konstruktionen in der Psychoanalyse*, ed. G. Kimmerle (Tübingen, 1998).

20. Yerushalmi, *Freud's Moses*, 21–22, has collated the relevant passages from Freud's letters and the book itself.

21. Freud mentions the hypothesis that the Jewish name for god "Adonai" ("my lord"), which takes the place of the inexpressible tetragram, goes back to the name Aten, the god of Akhenaten, but thankfully he does not pursue this any further.

22. O. H. Steck, *Israel und das gewaltsame Geschick der Propheten* (Neukirchen-Vluyn, 1967).

23. Freud is here following a theory proposed by the Old Testament scholar Ernst Sellin, *Mose und seine Bedeutung für die Israelitisch-jüdische Religionsgeschichte* (Leipzig, 1922), which was later retracted by Sellin.

24. Freud first presented and expanded on the following theory in *Totem and Taboo*, particularly in the fourth essay, "The Return of Totemism in Childhood." Freud, *Totem and Taboo*, in *Origins of Religion*, 43–224.

25. Freud, *Moses and Monotheism*, 346–47.

26. Ibid., 344–45.

27. Freud, *Moses and Monotheism*, 347. See Goldstein, *Reinscribing Moses*, 117, and Yerushalmi, *Freud's Moses*, 30.

28. Freud, *Moses and Monotheism*, 359–60.

29. Ibid., 360.

30. On the biblical ban on graven images, see chapter 3, nn. 25, 27, and 28, above.

31. Hecataeus of Abdera *Aigyptiaka*, excerpts in Diodorus *Bibl. hist.* 40.3 = *Diodorus of Sicily*, ed. and trans. F. R. Walton, Loeb Classical Library (Cambridge, Mass., 1967), 283; see also Menachem Stern, *Greek and Latin Authors on Jews and Judaism*, 3 vols. (Jerusalem, 1974–84), 1: 20–44, and G. C. Hansen, "Der Judenexkurs des Hekataios und die Folgen," in *Internationales Josephus-Kolloquium*, ed. J. U. Kalms (Aarhus, 1999; Münster 2000), 11–12; B. Bar-Kochva, *Pseudo-Hecataeus, On the Jews: Legitimizing the Jewish Diaspora* (Berkeley, 1996).

32. Strabo is arguing here along the lines of a widespread theology that held the cosmos to be god's temple. This is an argument against the cult of images that misses the point of the biblical ban on graven images. *There* it is a matter of remaining true to the one god; images are synonymous with "other gods." *Here* image-making is attacked because it inappropriately reduces the all-encompassing, sensuously inaccessible cosmos (the logos that rules the universe can only be grasped by the understanding, not by the senses) to the dimensions of a concrete cultic object. It is assumed that Strabo is drawing on Poseidonius here, hence that the substance of the text dates back to the mid-second century BCE.

33. Strabo *Geographica* 16.2.35; Stern, *Greek and Latin Authors*, 1: 261–351, esp. 300.

34. See Assmann, *Moses the Egyptian*, 91–96.

35. Tacitus, *Historiae* 5.5.4 = Stern, *Greek and Latin Authors*, 2: 26. On the high regard in which many Greeks held the Jewish idea of god and its supposed philosophical abstraction, see Martin Hengel, *Judentum und Hellenismus*, 3rd ed. (Tübingen, 1988), chap. 4.

36. Freud, *Moses and Monotheism*, 308.

37. Karl Jaspers, *Vom Ursprung und Ziel der Geschichte* (Munich, 1949). On Jaspers's theory of a general breakthrough to transcendence around 500 BCE, see Introduction, n. 3, above.

38. Freud, *Moses and Monotheism*, 362–63. In the original version: "the alternative that was more significant culturally."

39. I should emphasize that I am consciously operating here at the level of the cultural-typological clichés that informed Freud's thinking, and not at the level of historical research, which sets out precisely to deconstruct such clichés. My aim is not to correct Freud as an historian but to understand why he disregarded rival conceptions that, like his own, viewed the development of humankind as a progress in intellectuality, but located the decisive breakthroughs elsewhere.

40. Freud, *Moses and Monotheism*, 328, 332: "We have already said that the Christian ceremony of Holy Communion, in which the believer incorporates the Saviour's blood and flesh, repeats the content of the old totem meal—no doubt

only in its affectionate meaning, expressive of veneration, and not in its aggressive meaning."

41. D. Boyarin, *Carnal Israel: Reading Sex in Talmudic Culture* (Berkeley, 1993).

42. Freud, *Moses and Monotheism*, 385.

43. Ibid., 332–33.

44. Ibid., 365.

45. See Hans G. Kippenberg, *Die Entdeckung der Religionsgeschichte* (Munich, 1997), 218–43.

46. See Odo Casel, "Die *logikē thysia* der antiken Mystik in der christlich-liturgischen Umdeutung," *Jahrbuch für Liturgiewissenschaft* 4 (1924): 37–47. Treatise XIII of the *Corpus Hermeticum* is the most important text here; see W. Grese, *Corpus Hermeticum XIII and Early Christian Literature* (Leiden, 1979).

47. Hermann Cohen, *Religion of Reason out of the Sources of Israel*, trans. Simon Kaplan (New York, 1972).

48. See Jan Assmann, "In Bilder verstrickt: Bildkult, Idolatrie und Kosmotheismus in der Antike," in *Metapher und Wirklichkeit: Die Logik der Bildhaftigkeit im Reden von Gott, Mensch und Natur*, ed. Reinhold Bernhardt and Ulrike Link-Wieczorek (Göttingen, 1999), 73–88.

CHAPTER 5

1. See Carsten Colpe, "Sakralisierung von Texten und Filiationen von Kanons," in *Kanon und Zensur*, ed. Aleida Assmann and Jan Assmann (Munich, 1987), 80–92.

2. Moses Mendelssohn, *Jerusalem, Or, On Religious Power and Judaism*, trans. Allan Arkush (Hanover, N.H., 1983), 104.

3. See Jan Assmann, "Pictures versus Letters: William Warburton's Theory of Grammatological Iconoclasm," in *Representation in Religion: Studies in Honor of Moshe Barasch*, ed. Jan Assmann and Albert I. Baumgarten (Leiden, 2001), 297–311.

4. See Jan Assmann, *Das kulturelle Gedächtnis: Schrift, Erinnerung und politische Identität in frühen Hochkulturen* (Munich, 1992), 87–103.

5. A. Dihle, "Heilig," in *Reallexikon für Antike und Christentum: Sachwörterbuch zur Auseinandersetzung des Christentums mit der Antiken Welt*, ed. Ernst Dassmann et al., vol. 14 (Stuttgart, 1988), 1–63. Greek and Latin distinguish two concepts of the sacred, which are conflated in Hebrew as well as in modern languages. One word, *hieros* in Greek, *sacer* in Latin, denotes "the sacred as it is objectively brought to presence in many places," the other, *hosios* and *sanctus*, designates "the human qualifications or circumstances necessary for communicating with the sa-

cred" (A. Dihle, "Buch und Kult," unpublished MS. I thank Albrecht Dihle for sharing this text with me.)

6. Mendelssohn, *Jerusalem*, 104.

7. Flavius Josephus, *Josephus*, vol. 1: *The Life* [and] *Against Apion*, trans. H. St. J. Thackeray, Loeb Classical Library (1926; Cambridge, Mass., 2004), 369.

8. See esp. Moshe Halbertal, *People of the Book: Canon, Meaning, and Authority* (Cambridge, Mass., 1997).

9. Friedrich Kittler, "Die Heilige Schrift," in *Das Heilige: Seine Spur in der Moderne*, ed. D. Kamper and Ch. Wulf (Frankfurt, 1987), 154–62, quotation from p. 154.

10. Theo Sundermeier, "Religion, Religions" (cited in Introduction, n. 1, above), 392.

11. See H. Cancik and H. Mohr, "Erinnerung/Gedächtnis," in *Handwörterbuch religionswissenschaftlicher Grundbegriffe*, 2 vols. (Stuttgart, 1990), 1: 299–323.

12. Sara Stroumsa, "Entre Harran et al-Maghreb: Le théorie maimonidienne de l'histoire des religions et ses sources arabes," in *Judiós y musulmanes en al-Andalus y el Maghreb, contactos intelectuales*, ed. Maribel Fierro (Madrid, 2002), 153–64.

13. Harald Weinrich, in *Lethe: Kunst und Kritik des Vergessens* (Munich, 1997), and *Gibt es eine Kunst des Vergessens?* (Basel, 1996), argues against Eco for the existence of an art of forgetting. However, Weinrich only discusses individual forgetting, whereas the theory of normative inversion scholarship pioneered in the discipline of religious studies relates to collective forgetting.

14. John Spencer, *De legibus Hebraeorum ritualibus et earum rationibus* (1685), 1: 155. Evgen Tarantul draws my attention to Isaiah 40:2 for the rare form *kfilayim*, "reduplication," "double" ("for she hath received of the Lord's hand double for all her sins"). Spencer's Hebrew is not punctuated. The adjective *kfulîm*, "double," corresponding to "duplicata," requires, of course, *dvarîm* instead of the *status constructus divrej.*

15. Theo Sundermeier, "Religion, Religionen," 411–23; see also id., *Was ist Religion? Religionswissenschaft im theologischen Kontext* (Gütersloh, 1999).

16. Sundermeier, "Religion, Religionen," 418.

17. See *Die Erfindung des Inneren Menschen: Studien zur religiösen Anthropologie*, ed. Jan Assmann and Theo Sundermeier (Gütersloh, 1993).

18. The language of this commandment derives from the Hethitic and Assyrian loyalty oaths, as Moshe Weinfeld, "The Loyalty Oath in the Ancient Near East," *Ugaritische Forschungen* 8 (1976): 379–414, has shown, e.g.: "As you love your wives, your children and your dwellings, so you should love everything related to the king"; "If you do not love Assurbanipal as your own life"; "If the life of our lord is not more valuable to us than our own" (ibid., 384, Hethitic officers' oath).

19. Emanuel bin Gorion [Emanuel Berdyczewski], *Die Sagen der Juden*, 5 vols. (Frankfurt, 1913–23), 1: xi.

20. Iamblichus *De mysteriis* 8.2. See J. Assmann, *Re und Amun: Die Krise des polytheistischen Weltbilds im Ägypten der 18.-20. Dynastie* (Fribourg, 1983), 171–75.

21. Thomas Mann, *Joseph and His Brothers*, trans. Helen Lowe-Porter (Harmondsworth, UK, 1978), 589.

22. [Gerhard Kaiser, "War der Exodus den Sündenfall?" in Assmann, *Mosaische Unterscheidung*, 244.—Trans.]

23. Mann, *Joseph and His Brothers*, trans. Lowe-Porter, 754.

CONCLUSION

1. [Karl-Josef Kuschel, "Moses, Monotheismus und die Kultur der Moderne," in Assmann, *Mosaische Unterscheidung*, 275.—Trans.]

2. [Kuschel, "Moses, Monotheismus und die Kultur der Moderne," 279.—Trans.]

3. Michael Rißmann, *Hitlers Gott: Vorsehungsglaube und Sendungsbewußtsein des deutschen Diktators* (Zurich, 2001). In his discussion of this book in *Die Welt*, 25 August 2001, Hannes Stein suggested that Hitler's religion be classified as "cosmotheism."

4. See, e.g., Wouter J. Hanegraaf, *New Age Religion and Western Culture: Esotericism in the Mirror of Secular Thought* (Albany, N.Y., 1998), and *Nature Religion Today: Paganism in the Modern World*, ed. Joanne Pearson, Richard H. Roberts, and Geoffrey Samuel (Edinburgh, 1998).